THE BIBLE
AND
BIRTH CONTROL

I remember a great man coming into my house, at Waltham, and seeing all my children standing in the order of their age and stature, said, "These are they that make rich men poor." But he straight received this answer, "Nay, my lord, these are they that make a poor man rich; for there is not one of these whom we would part with for all your wealth."

Joseph Hall, 1574-1656

THE BIBLE
AND
BIRTH CONTROL

by
CHARLES D. PROVAN

ZIMMER PRINTING
410 WEST MAIN STREET
MONONGAHELA, PENNSYLVANIA 15063
U.S.A.

Published by Zimmer Printing
410 West Main Street, Monongahela, Pennsylvania 15063 U.S.A.

TABLE OF CONTENTS

Introduction

Author's Note

Acknowledgements

CHAPTER ONE
Nine Reasons Why the Bible Prohibits Birth Control
(Pages 1 through 32)

CHAPTER TWO
Two Alternate Viewpoints on Birth Control and Their Rebuttals
(Pages 33 through 60)

CHAPTER THREE
Protestant Theologians and the Onan Incident
(Pages 61 through 98)

INTRODUCTION

When I first encountered the question: "Is the practice of birth control acceptable in God's sight?" I responded with typical 20th century arrogance and "wisdom" -- sure it is! But through this book and personal conversations with the author I have been challenged to rethink some very basic issues: Does the Bible approve of birth control? What are God's purposes for marriage? Are children a blessing as the Bible says or an expensive liability? Is God really sovereign in childbirth? Does He really open and close the womb? Can He take care of people if He blesses them with a large family?

I was forced to go back to the Bible and to prayerfully consider these questions. Here I think the reader will find this book helpful. The author's exegesis is careful and thorough. Although we do not see eye to eye on everything, he has shown me that the teachings of Scripture are clearer than I had anticipated on many important points: God is sovereign not just in salvation, but also in providing a couple with children; children are a blessing and many children are a great blessing. I was surprised to see how much our culture's thinking had affected my reading of Scripture. Finally, as the witnesses from history began speaking out, I realized that the blinders of our modern day pragmatism had stopped me from seeing God's Word clearly and considering the subject honestly.

Let me challenge my fellow readers to give the author a hearing. Don't bring up your objections too quickly ("Oh, the Onan passage can't mean that"), don't panic too quickly ("Oh no, I'll have 17 children" or "what will our parents think"), guard against your unbelief ("Oh, we will starve") and trust God. There is an important message for God's people in this book. It goes against much of what the world thinks is wise and prudent. But God's ways are not our ways.

It is my hope that this book will begin to lead us back to God's ways in this area. To value what God values - children. To recognize His sovereignty - He knows best how many children we should have. And to trust Him to work His will, provision, and protection in our lives. I am grateful that the author had the insight and courage to challenge me to seek the Lord in this matter. May God bless you as you take time to consider His will in this important aspect of His creation. May He be glorified as His people affirm:

> "Behold, children are a gift of the Lord;
> The fruit of the womb is a reward.
> Like arrows in the hand of a warrior,
> So are the children of one's youth.
> How blessed is the man whose quiver is full of them."

Psalm 127:3 - 5 (NASB)

Pastor Todd Jaussen
Donora, Pennsylvania
March, 1989

Author's Note

Chapter One of this book, "Nine Reasons Why the Bible Prohibits Birth Control", is a somewhat revised edition of an article entitled "The Bible's View of Birth Control". This article appeared in the *Christian News* of February 29, 1988. The *Christian News* is a theologically conservative newspaper with mainly a Lutheran outlook. Though this Lutheran outlook dominates the newspaper, it provides a non-censored forum for many differing views, and contains many articles of interest to those who believe the Bible. For information on the *Christian News,* please write to: *Christian News,* P.O. Box 168, New Haven, Missouri 63068. The article is reprinted here with the permission of Charles D. Provan (myself!) and Pastor Herman Otten, editor of the *Christian News.*

Chapter Two, "Two Alternate Viewpoints on Birth Control, and Rebuttals of the Same", contains two responses to my article (both of which were printed by *Christian News*) and my responses to them. The first alternate, "Another View On Onan", was anonymously signed "A Concerned Friend". The second, entitled "Devil's Advocate", was composed by Pastor Roger Kovaciny of Columbus, Ohio. Permission to reprint these two responses was graciously given by Pastor Otten (in lieu of "A Concerned Friend") and Pastor Kovaciny. Because the "Devil's Advocate" article is long and makes a number of points, I have added paragraph numbers for ease of reference. The Scripture quotes in my rebuttals are primarily from the New International Version of the Bible.

Chapter Three, "Protestant Theologians and the Onan Incident", was compiled in order to demonstrate the fact that the Protestant view of the Biblical account of Onan has always been (till the corrupt Twentieth Century) that Onan was killed for unnatural sexual relations with his wife, a point which has direct bearing upon Birth Control.

Charles D. Provan
Monongahela, Pennsylvania
March, 1989

ACKNOWLEDGMENTS

During the compilation of this manuscript I have been helped by a sizable number of institutions and people. I am very grateful to them all, and would like to take this opportunity to thank the most prominent:

The Staff of the Clifford E. Barbour Library at the Pittsburgh Theological Seminary, Pittsburgh, Pennsylvania (especially Stephen Crocco and Jayne Schneider)

The Staff of Concordia Seminary Library, St. Louis, Missouri (particularly Mike Awe and Tim Engel)

Reformed Presbyterian Theological Seminary Library, Pittsburgh, Pennsylvania

(Let me say in passing that the rare book collections contained in the above libraries are veritable treasure troves of godly teaching -- we highly recommend them to one and all.)

Werner Barbye* (and his wife)
Ford Battles*
Kelly DelTredici*
Jim and Lisa Dodson
John Drickamer*
Walter Hibbard
Todd Jaussen

Dave Kudlik
Philip Long*
Lawrence Marquardt
Herman Otten
Tim Otten
Carol Provan

A special word goes to those whose names are followed by an asterisk, my translators. They put up with phone calls and letters above and beyond the call of duty in helping me to locate and translate passages which were of peculiar interest to me! Many thanks.

CHAPTER ONE

NINE REASONS WHY THE BIBLE PROHIBITS BIRTH CONTROL

by Charles D. Provan

For this word which God spreaks, "Be fruitful and multiply," is not a command. It is more than a command, namely, a divine ordinance [werck] which it is not our prerogative to hinder or ignore. Rather, it is just as necessary as the fact that I am a man, and more necessary than sleeping and waking, eating and drinking, and emptying the bowels and bladder. It is a nature and disposition just as innate as the organs involved in it. Therefore, just as God does not command anyone to be a man or a woman but creates them the way they have to be, so he does not command them to multiply but creates them so that they have to multiply. And wherever men try to resist this, it remains irresistible nonetheless and goes its way through fornication, adultery, and secret sins, for this is a matter of nature and not of choice.

In the third place, from this ordinance of creation God has himself exempted three categories of men, saying in Matthew 19 [:12], "There are eunuchs who have been so from birth, and there are eunuchs who have been made eunuchs by men, and there are eunuchs who have made themselves eunuchs for the sake of the kingdom of heaven." Apart from these three groups, let no man presume to be without a spouse. And whoever does not fall within one of these three categories should not consider anything except the estate of marriage. Otherwise it is simply impossible for you to remain righteous. For the Word of God which created you and said, "Be fruitful and multiply", abides and rules within you; you can by no means ignore it, or you will be bound to commit heinous sins without end.

Martin Luther

INTRODUCTION TO
CHAPTER ONE

By Charles D. Provan

Many Christians today have not even considered the question, "What does God think of birth control?" It is a question "too stupid to even consider" in the eyes of most. After all, birth control is an American social custom, practised by most married couples in our country, and in most "civilized countries," too.

But just because Americans think that birth control is morally acceptable does not make birth control right in the eyes of God. Our study here will seek to lay a solid Biblical basis for opposition to birth control. You may be surprised to find that the Bible does in fact say quite a bit about this widespread custom -- all of it negative. What we say here should not be viewed as a new idea, for it is a fact that the Christian Church, since its inception, has consistently opposed birth control as a great evil. This opposition continued quite strongly down into this present century, when birth control carried the day. Some theologians spoke out against the limiting of children by Christians until fairly recent times. And now, opposition to birth control is almost dead. We hope this paper will help to rekindle it, and lead to God bestowing many blessings upon his people: wonderful children!

Before you begin, please be aware of the fact that this paper quotes quite a few Scripture verses which mention sexual matters. We have not used these verses to offend people, but have used them to illustrate various points in our argument. Please do not become upset. Rather, understand that the Bible speaks plainly of these matters. Many do not realize that all the members of Israel, including children, were commanded to hear the entire Mosaic Law. This law contains many blunt statements on sex, things about which all Israel was to be informed. And this is why we feel free to talk about them, in a proper manner.

Some may think that we quote the Old Testament too much. However, we do not feel badly about this, since the New Testament itself contains some sixteen hundred references to the Old Testament. Further, the Church of Christ is "built upon the foundation of the apostles and prophets," as Paul says in Ephesians 2:20. In addition, in 1 Corinthians 5:1, Paul gets his rules on sexual matters right out of the Mosaic Law (Lev. 18:8), and he was writing to converted Gentiles! As Martin Luther says, God gave us his holy Law "to keep men from open outbreaks of sin" and to "teach us the works which are really pleasing to God." (Small Catechism, Question 159).

3

All Scripture quotes in this chapter are from the New American Standard Version of the Bible. A few of the verses we have cited are margin translations of the same version.

REASON NUMBER ONE

BE FRUITFUL AND MULTIPLY

(GENESIS 1:27-28)

Genesis 1:27-28
"27. And God created man in His own image, in the image of God He created him; male and female He created them. 28. And God blessed them; and God said to them, 'Be fruitful and multiply, and fill the earth, and subdue it; and rule over the fish of the sea and over the birds of the sky, and over every living thing that moves on the earth.'"

Christians should take note of the fact that the first listed command to mankind was "Be fruitful and multiply." This command is repeated over again in the Bible several times (for instance, in Genesis 9:1 and 35:11). Our point is this: this is a command of God, indeed the first command to a married couple. Birth control obviously involves disobedience to this command, for birth control attempts to prevent being fruitful and multiplying. Therefore birth control is wrong, because it involves disobedience to the Word of God. Nowhere is this command done away with in the entire Bible; therefore it still remains valid for us today.

Martin Luther had this to say in regard to Genesis 1:28: "He has created male and female and has blessed them that they might be fruitful." (Luther's Works, Vol. 5, p. 329)

On this same occasion Luther said, "...fertility was regarded as an extraordinary blessing and a special gift of God, as is clear from Deut. 28:4, where Moses numbers fertility among the blessings. 'There will not be a barren woman among you,' he says (cf. Ex. 23:26). We do not regard this so highly today. Although we like and desire it in cattle, yet in the human race there are few who regard a woman's fertility as a blessing. Indeed, there are many who have an aversion for it and regard sterility as a special blessing. Surely this is also contrary to nature. Much less is it pious and saintly. For this affection has been implanted by God in man's nature, so that it desires its increase and multiplication. Accordingly, it is inhuman and godless to have a loathing for offspring. Thus someone recently called his wife a sow, since she gave birth rather often. The good for nothing and impure fellow! The saintly fathers did

5

not feel like this at all; for they acknowledged a fruitful wife as a special blessing of God and, on the other hand, regarded sterility as a curse. And this judgment flowed from the Word of God in Gen. 1:28, where He said: 'Be fruitful and multiply.' From this they understood that children are a gift of God." (Luther's Works, Vol. 5, p. 325).

In Matthew 19:1-9, Jesus was questioned by the Pharisees concerning marriage and divorce. The Pharisees allowed divorce for a multitude of stupid reasons. Jesus corrected their view by calling their attention to Gen. 1:27 and 2:24, telling the Pharisees that if they wanted to see what God wanted in a marriage, they should get their rules from the way God set up marriage in "the beginning." Please note that marriage as invented by God "in the beginning" was set up to "be fruitful and multiply" -- NOT to "be sterile" !

Many today will say, "But I cannot afford to have lots of children, and so I must practise birth control. If I don't, I will be poor, and my children will be stuck in grinding poverty." Listen to what Martin Luther has to say on this subject: "Although it is very easy to marry a wife, it is very difficult to support her along with the children and the household. Accordingly, no one notices this faith of Jacob. Indeed, many hate fertility in a wife for the sole reason that the offspring must be supported and brought up. For this is what they commonly say: 'Why should I marry a wife when I am a pauper and a beggar? I would rather bear the burden of poverty alone and not load myself with misery and want.' But this blame is unjustly fastened on marriage and fruitfulness. Indeed, you are indicting your unbelief by distrusting God's goodness, and you are bringing greater misery upon yourself by disparaging God's blessing. For if you had trust in God's grace and promises, you would undoubtedly be supported. But because you do not hope in the Lord, you will never prosper." (Luther's Works, Vol. 5, p. 332).

We Christians worship the great and powerful Lord who created the entire world. Can we truly believe that if we obey Him in this matter of being fruitful and multiplying, He will desert us? This idea is truly foreign to the Bible. God is not obligated to give us a Cadillac, but He promises to give us food and clothing and shelter. (Psa. 37:25 says, "I have been young, and now I am old; Yet I have not seen the righteous forsaken, Or his descendants begging bread." And Jesus says in Mat. 6:33, "But seek first His kingdom and His righteousness; and all these things shall be added to you.") Our dedication to God should be that of Daniel's three friends, who said, "...our God whom we serve is able to deliver us from the furnace of blazing fire; and He will deliver us out of your hand, O king. But even if he does not, let it be known to you, O king, that we are not going to serve your gods or worship the golden image that you have set up." (Dan. 3:17-18)

REASON NUMBER TWO

CHILDREN ARE A BLESSING FROM GOD: THE MORE THE BETTER!

(PSALM 127:3-5, 1 CHRONICLES 25:4-5 & 26:4-5)

Psalm 127:3-5
"3. Behold, children are a gift of the Lord; the fruit of the womb is a reward. 4. Like arrows in the hand of a warrior, so are the children of one's youth. 5. How blessed is the man whose quiver is full of them; they shall not be ashamed, when they speak with their enemies in the gate."

1 Chronicles 25:4-5
"4. Of Heman, the sons of Heman: Bukkiah, Mattaniah, Uzziel, Shebuel and Jerimoth, Hananiah, Hanani, Eliathah, Giddalti and Romamti-ezer, Josh-bekashah, Mallothi, Hothir, Mahazioth. 5. All these were the sons of Heman the king's seer to exalt him according to the words of God, for God gave fourteen sons and three daughters to Heman."

1 Chronicles 26:4-5
"4. And Obed-edom had sons: Shemaiah the first-born, Jehozabad the second, Joah the third, Sacar the fourth, Nethanel the fifth, 5. Ammiel the sixth, Issachar the seventh, and Peullethai the eighth; God had indeed blessed him."

According to Holy Scripture in Psa. 127:5, "How blessed is the man whose quiver is full of them." Children (the more the better) are a blessing from God. What this has to do with birth control is plain to see: for birth control seeks to prevent children from being conceived, thereby preventing children from being born. This act prevents blessings of God from being given to people. Lest there be those who would say, "those kinds of blessings I don't want," let us recall the story about Esau in Gen. 25:29-34. God gave Esau a blessing (his birthright), and Esau sold it to his brother Jacob for a bowl of stew! Genesis says that by this act Esau "despised" the blessing of God. What does Hebrews 12:16 have to say about Esau? It says that Esau was "a godless person... who sold his own birthright for a single meal." Christians of today have been so influenced by our godless materialistic culture that their view of children is the same as that of the world: "children are an economic drain -- they make you poor -- they limit economic progress -- they prevent women from reaching their potential." This is not what the Bible says. The

Bible says in 1 Chron. 25:5 that "God gave fourteen sons and three daughters to Heman" "to exalt him." (It does not say, "to degrade him" or "to make him disgustingly poor", which is what our modern birth control advocates might have written, had they and not the Holy Spirit been in charge of writing the Bible!) The Holy Spirit also wrote in 1 Chron. 26:5 that "God had indeed blessed" Obed-edom by giving him eight sons! Planned Parenthood or some of our modern so-called "Christian Sex Manuals" might have used Obed-edom as a horror story for "overpopulation."

By the way, I have heard of people who say that they have a "quiver full of children" by having three or five children "because back in ancient times that was how many arrows soldiers carried in their quivers." I am not aware of the source of this amazing and ridiculous viewpoint, which may be over-thrown "out of the mouths of babes and sucklings." Just go up to a little boy or girl and ask them this question: "If you were a soldier, and you were going to be in a battle with the fierce enemy, how many arrows would you put in your quiver?" The answer will be "piles and piles of arrows" or "bunches and bunches of arrows." So children can interpret Psalm 127:4-5 better than people who already are in favor of birth control. "Like arrows in the hand of a warrior, so are the children of one's youth. How blessed is the man whose quiver is full of them..." Which passage obviously means that the more chil-dren a believing couple has, the better. The amount of children with which a couple is blessed should be determined by God, not birth control. Dr. Luther had this to say concerning Psa. 127: "This passage [Gen. 9:1], moreover, leads us to believe that children are a gift of God and come solely through the blessing of God, just as Ps. 127:3 shows. The heathen, who have not been instructed by the Word of God, believe that the propagation of the human race happens partly by nature, partly by accident, especially since those who are regarded as most suited for procreation often fail to have children. Therefore the heathen do not thank God for this gift, nor do they receive their children as the gift of God." (Luther's Works, Vol. 2, p. 132) If Martin Luther was alive today, would he not disapprove of many Christians who view children as a bad thing, and so practise birth control to prevent God from sending more blessings to them? If God wanted to bless Christians by sending them a house to live in, would people practise "house-control" and refuse the house? We think not. And we are not aware of any people who would turn down God if he wanted to reward them with money, either. But when it comes to children, Christian principles change as if by magic! But truly Scriptural principles do not change at all: therefore Christians should willingly receive the blessings which God has for us, and not try to prevent them.

REASON NUMBER THREE

CHILDLESSNESS IS AN UNFORTUNATE THING

(HOSEA 9:10-17, EXODUS 23:25-26,

DEUTERONOMY 7:13-14)

Hosea 9:10-17
"10. I found Israel like grapes in the wilderness; I saw your forefathers as the earliest fruit on the fig tree in its first season. But they came to Baal-peor and devoted themselves to shame, and they became as detestable as that which they loved. 11. As for Ephraim, their glory will fly away like a bird - no birth, no pregnancy, and no conception! 12. Though they bring up their children, yet I will bereave them until not a man is left. Yes, woe to them indeed when I depart from them! 13. Ephraim, as I have seen, is planted in a pleasant meadow like Tyre; but Ephraim will bring out his children for slaughter. 14. Give them, O Lord - what wilt Thou give? Give them a miscarrying womb and dry breasts. 15. All their evil is at Gilgal; indeed, I came to hate them there! Because of the wickedness of their deeds I will drive them out of My house! I will love them no more; all their princes are rebels. 16. Ephraim is stricken, their root is dried up, they will bear no fruit. Even though they bear children, I will slay the precious ones of their womb. 17. My God will cast them away because they have not listened to Him; and they will be wanderers among the nations."

Exodus 23:25-26
"25. But you shall serve the LORD your God, and He will bless your bread and your water; and I will remove sickness from your midst. 26. There shall be no one miscarrying or barren in your land; I will fulfill the number of your days."

Deuteronomy 7:13-14
"13. And He will love you and bless you and multiply you; He will also bless the fruit of your womb and the fruit of your ground, your grain and your new wine and your oil, the increase of your herd and the young of your flock, in the land which He swore to your forefathers to give you. 14. You shall be blessed above all peoples; there shall be no male or female barren among you or among your cattle."

When God decided to punish the corrupt nation of Israel some twenty-six hundred years ago, how did he do it? He prevented conception, pregnancy and childbirth, and killed the children who survived. God views childlessness or less children than possible as a negative occurrence, something which he uses as a punishment. Doesn't it say a lot about our dying and impotent culture, which welcomes birth control (with its resultant few or no children) as a "great scientific achievement" and a "blessing to mankind." Birth control brings about a lamentable catastrophe according to the Bible!

Commenting on Genesis 17, Luther had this to say about sterility, "...saintly women have always regarded childbirth as a great sign of grace. Rachel is rude and exceedingly irksome to her husband when she says (Gen. 30:1): 'Give me children, or I shall die!' She makes it clear that she will die of grief because she sees that barrenness is a sign of wrath. And in Ps. 127:3 there is a glorious eulogy of offspring: 'Lo, sons are a heritage from the Lord, the fruit of the womb a reward (that is, a gift of God).' Surely it is a magnificent name that children are the gift of God! Therefore Hannah laments so pitiably (1 Sam. 1:10), and John's aged mother Elizabeth leaps for joy and exults (Luke 1:25): 'The Lord has taken away my reproach.' Thus when the world was still in a better state, barrenness was considered a sign of wrath; but childbirth was considered a sign of grace. Because of the abuses of lust, however, this remnant of the divine blessing gradually began to be obscured even among the Jews, just as today you could find many greedy men who regard numerous offspring as a punishment. Saintly mothers, however, have always regarded this gift -- when they were prolific -- as a great honor, just as, conversely, they have regarded barrenness as a sign of wrath and as a reproach." (Luther's Works, Vol. 3, p. 134-135)

Moving on to the other Scripture passages in our list, we can see that God promised great blessings to Israel, among them (Exo. 23:25-26) the negation of sickness, miscarriages and barrenness. Christians and heathen both view sickness as a bad thing, and Christians view miscarriages (at least caused miscarriages, that is, abortions) as bad. But when it comes to deliberately causing one's own sterility (whether temporary or permanent, via birth control), most Christians unite with the heathen and declare sterility a good thing! As for Moses, he seems to view sickness, miscarriages and sterility as bad.

In Deuteronomy 7:12-13, it gets more pointed. Moses says, "God will love you and bless you and multiply you; He will also bless the fruit of your womb.... You shall be blessed above all peoples; there shall be no male or female barren among you...." Once again, we see barrenness, male or female, as a bad thing. Since barrenness is a bad and undesirable thing, so is birth control, since birth control is temporary or permanent sterility.

Yet, in our culture, barrenness is "no big deal", and people are always attempting to tell sterile couples that "everything is all right." But everything is not all right! Listen to what Martin Luther had to say, commenting upon Rachel's great desire to have children: "...from this it is clear that the very saintly women were not lustful but were desirous of offspring and the blessing. For this was the cause of envy in Rachel, who, if she had been like other women whom our age has produced in large numbers, would have said: 'What is it to me whether I bear children or not? Provided that I remain the mother of the household and have an abundance of all other things, I have enough.' But Rachel demands offspring so much that she prefers death to remaining sterile. I do not remember reading a similar statement in any history. Therefore she is an example of a very pious and continent woman whose only zeal and burning desire is for offspring, even if it means death. Thus above (Gen. 16:2) Sarah also showed a similar desire for offspring. And in both this feeling is decidedly praiseworthy. 'If I do not have children, I shall die' says Rachel. 'I prefer being without life to being without children.' ...Consequently, she determines either to bear children or die. Thus later she dies in childbirth. This desire and feeling of the godly woman is good and saintly...." (Luther's Works, Vol. 5, p. 328)

REASON NUMBER FOUR

THE ONAN INCIDENT

(GEN. 38:8-10, DEU. 25:5-10)

Genesis 38:8-10
"8. Then Judah said to Onan, 'Go in to your brother's wife, and perform your duty as a brother-in-law to her, and raise up offspring for your brother.' 9. And Onan knew that the offspring would not be his; so it came about that when he went in to his brother's wife, he wasted his seed on the ground, in order not to give offspring to his brother. 10. But what he did was displeasing in the sight of the LORD; so He took his life also."

Deuteronomy 25:5-10
"5. When brothers live together and one of them dies and has no son, the wife of the deceased shall not be married outside the family to a strange man. Her husband's brother shall go in to her and take her to himself as wife and perform the duty of a husband's brother to her. 6. And it shall be that the first-born whom she bears shall assume the name of his dead brother, that his name may not be blotted out from Israel. 7. But if the man does not desire to take his brother's wife, then his brother's wife shall go up to the gate to the elders and say, 'My husband's brother refuses to establish a name for his brother in Israel; he is not willing to perform the duty of a husband's brother to me.' 8. Then the elders of his city shall summon him and speak to him. And if he persists and says, 'I do not desire to take her,' 9. then his brother's wife shall come to him in the sight of the elders, and pull his sandal off his foot and spit in his face; and she shall declare, 'Thus it is done to the man who does not build up his brother's house.' 10. And in Israel his name shall be called, 'The house of him whose sandal is removed.'"

Judah had several sons. The oldest son, named Er, had been married, but was killed by God before he had any children. In accordance with the law of God in Deu. 25:5-10, Judah told his next son Onan to marry Er's widow, so as to produce a child who would carry on Er's name.

However, Onan was unwilling to father a child for his deceased brother, so "when he went in to his brother's wife, he wasted his seed on the ground." A few words later we read, "But what he did was displeasing in the sight of the Lord; so He took his life also."

Examine the above verses and ask yourself this question: "What did Onan do in the verses?" The only thing Onan did in the verses was "wasted

12

his seed on the ground." That is what made God angry. If there wasn't such a stir at this obvious conclusion we could drop the matter here, but we can't do so, because those who defend birth control have come up with alternatives which suit their views. We shall now review three alternate explanations, and show why they are untenable.

ALTERNATE #1: "Onan was killed by God for disobeying his father, not for wasting his seed."

REBUTTAL: According to Scripture, God has decreed that the marriage of a son ends any mandatory obedience to his father. Genesis 2:24 says, "For this cause a man shall leave his father and his mother, and shall cleave unto his wife; and they shall become one flesh." So, if Judah had authority over Onan, his authority ended when Onan got married to his brother's widow. Therefore God did not kill Onan because he disobeyed Judah, because according to the word of God, Onan did not have to obey him.

ALTERNATE #2: "Onan was killed by God because he didn't show love for his brother by having a child. He should have had at least one child before practising birth control, and then God wouldn't have been angry."

REBUTTAL: Deuteronomy eliminates this reason as a possibility, because it says that regardless of a man's motives for refusing to raise up seed for a dead brother, the man is not to be put to death. He is to be humiliated only (shoe pulled off, face spit on, etc.). Onan was put to death for what he did, while the man in Deu. 25 is not.

As we compare the two Bible texts (Gen. 38:8-10 and Deu. 25:5-10), we need to ask, "What did Onan do that the man of Deu. 25 didn't do?" The difference in conduct will explain the difference in the penalty meted out by God. And the difference is that while Onan wasted his seed, the other man didn't! Suppose the man in Deu. 25 thinks exactly as Onan, saying to himself, "I don't want to raise up seed for my brother," and yet doesn't waste his seed? What happens to him according to the law of God? -- humiliation only, regardless of his unloving thoughts.

ALTERNATE #3: "Well, Onan must have been killed because he lied to Judah."

REBUTTAL: There is no proof that he lied to anyone. The Scripture is silent as to what Onan said to anyone. And we ought not to "go beyond what is written," as the apostle Paul says in 1 Cor. 4:6. The Holy Spirit says what Onan did, then it says that God killed him for what he did. And what he did was "waste his seed on the ground." Onan was killed because he "wasted seed." Therefore, birth control is automatically condemned, because all forms of birth control have as their goal the wasting of seed.

Some may say to themselves as they read this, "Why, this is just a Roman Catholic custom, and so may be discarded." But, dear readers, this is not so. Space restrictions prevent us from listing quotes from all the leaders of the Christian faith who agree with our interpretation of the Onan incident. (However, we do list the views of many Protestants, as well as Augustine, Epihanius and some others, in Chapter Three of our booklet.) We will here list the comments of Martin Luther and John Calvin, the founders of the Reformation, two pastors not known for advocating "mere Roman Catholic customs," as everyone knows.

Commenting on Genesis 38:8-10, Luther says, "Then Judah urged his son Onan to take Tamar for his wife to raise up seed to his brother. Moses here uses the Hebrew word "jabam," which we find also in Deuteronomy 25:5 and which properly means "to marry in order to beget children for the deceased brother." This was a very disagreeable duty and many sought to escape it, as we read in Ruth 4:1 ff., for it is indeed hard to live with a woman whom one does not love, to continue the inheritance of the brother, and to submit oneself to ceaseless toil and labor in his interest. Therefore Onan, unwilling to perform this obligation, spilled his seed. That was a sin far greater than adultery or incest, and it provoked God to such fierce wrath that He destroyed him immediately." (Luther's Commentary on Genesis, p. 250-251)

Luther on another occasion commented on the very same passage: "But the exceedingly foul deed of Onan, the basest of wretches, follows. [Here Luther quotes Gen. 38:9-10] Onan must have been a malicious and incorrigible scoundrel. This is a most disgraceful sin. It is far more atrocious than incest and adultery. We call it unchastity, yes a Sodomitic sin. For Onan goes in to her; that is, he lies with her and copulates, and when it comes to the point of insemination, spills the semen, lest the woman conceive. Surely at such a time the order of nature established by God in procreation shold be followed. Accordingly, it was a most disgraceful crime to produce semen and excite the woman, and to frustrate her at that very moment. He was inflamed with the basest spite and hatred. Therefore he did not allow himself to be compelled to bear that intolerable slavery. Consequently, he deserved to be killed by God. He committed an evil deed. Therefore God punished him. ...That worthless fellow....preferred polluting himself with a most disgraceful sin to raising up offspring for his brother." (Luther's Works, Vol. 7, p. 20-21)

Several years ago I purchased Calvin's Commentary on Genesis, to find out what Calvin thought of the Onan incident. Much to my surprise, when I opened to Genesis 38:8-10, I discovered that Calvin's comments on this pivotal birth control passage were omitted by the editor, for what reason he did not state. I was subsequently able to locate a Latin copy of Calvin's Commentary on Genesis, and the omitted section was graciously translated into Engish by the late Dr. Ford Battles, the translator of Calvin's Institutes. Calvin's comments are as follows:

"Besides, he [Onan; C.P.] not only defrauded his brother of the right due him, but also preferred his semen to putrify on the ground, rather than to beget a son in his brother's name. V. 10 The Jews quite immodestly gabble concerning this thing. It will suffice for me briefly to have touched upon this as much as modesty in speaking permits. The voluntary spilling of semen outside of intercourse between man and woman is a monstrous thing. Deliberately to withdraw from coitus in order that semen may fall on the ground is doubly monstrous. For this is to extinguish the hope of the race and to kill before he is born the hoped-for offspring. This impiety is especially condemned, now by the Spirit through Moses' mouth, that Onan, as it were, by a violent abortion, no less cruelly than filthily cast upon the ground the offspring of his brother, torn from the maternal womb. Besides, in this way he tried, as far as he was able, to wipe out a part of the human race. If any woman ejects a foetus from her womb by drugs, it is reckoned a crime incapable of expiation and deservedly Onan incurred upon himself the same kind of punishment, infecting the earth by his semen, in order that Tamar might not conceive a future human being as an inhabitant of the earth." (Calvin's Commentary on Genesis 38:8-10, translated from the Latin)

REASON NUMBER FIVE

DEATH PENALTIES FOR SEXUAL OFFENSES

(LEVITICUS 20:13,15,16,18, GENESIS 38:8-10)

Leviticus 20:13
"13. If there is a man who lies with a male as those who lie with a woman, both of them have committed a detestable act; they shall surely be put to death. Their bloodguiltiness is upon them."

Leviticus 20:15
"15. If there is a man who lies with an animal, he shall surely be put to death; you shall also kill the animal."

Leviticus 20:16
"16. If there is a woman who approaches any animal to mate with it, you shall kill the woman and the animal; they shall surely be put to death. Their bloodguiltiness is upon them."

Leviticus 20:18
"18. If there is a man who lies with a menstruous woman and uncovers her nakedness, he has laid bare her flow, and she has exposed the flow of her blood; thus both of them shall be cut off from among their people."

Genesis 38:8-10
(Listed under Reason Four)

The Old Testament mentions about twenty or so death penalty offenses. The New Testament says that these examples are in the Old Testament to help Christians find out what pleases and displeases God (1 Corinthians 10:1-10; verse 6 says, "Now these things happened as examples for us, that we should not crave evil things, as they also craved."). Many of these offenses are related to sexual matters. These forbidden sexual relations may be divided into two categories: a) sexual offenses forbidden because of who the potential or actual sexual partner is (for example, adultery, incest, etc.) and, b) offenses which are forbidden because of the act itself.

It is this second group on which we intend to focus. These offenses are evil no matter with whom they are committed. They are perversions, evil in themselves. A listing of these offenses is as follows:

1) Male homosexual intercourse (Lev. 20:13)
2) Male/Animal bestiality (Lev. 20:15)
3) Female/Animal bestiality (Lev. 20:16)
4) Intercourse with a menstrous woman (Lev. 20:18)
5) Withdrawal (Wasting Seed) (Gen. 38:8-10)

These sexual offenses are always wrong if done intentionally. (We say this because #4 and #5 may occur accidentally, as the Bible says -- Lev. 15:24 and Deu. 23:10-11.)

In any case let us get to the point of this section, which is this: What is common to all these five sins? The answer is: they are all sterile forms of sexual intercourse. Children cannot be produced from male homosexual activity or bestiality, even though seed is emitted. Menstrous intercourse is the most easily identified sterile time of the woman's monthly cycle. (Witness the important place menstruation plays in the "rhythm method".) Withdrawal is meant to be sterile, and is, most of the time. In all these cases the seed is wasted.

So we can see that the reason that these sins are condemned by God is because they are almost 100% sterile, and oppose the command of God to "be fruitful and multiply." We are not finished however, because further examination will be useful. Let us now compare some unusual cases of Old Testament jurisprudence.

Comparison Number One:
Male homosexuality vs. female homosexuality

Leviticus 20:13
"13. If there is a man who lies with a male as those who lie with a woman, both of them have committed a detestable act; they shall surely be put to death. Their bloodguiltiness is upon them."

The reader will note that we have included no verse on the execution of female homosexuals. This is because there is no penalty prescribed for lesbian activities in the Old Testament. This of course does not mean that lesbianism is OK with God -- it just means that there is no civil penalty. (Similar cases would be coveting or lusting, which are forbidden by God but have no civil penalty.) So we see that male homosexuals are to be executed, but female homosexuals are spared.

Some attempt the explanation that, "Well, God is just nicer to girls." We would reply that God in the Old Testament has nothing against executing female evildoers, as is evident from the fact that God has decreed the death penalty for: female murderers (Gen. 9:6), female sorcerers (Lev. 20:27), female idolators (Deu. 13:6-9), females guilty of bestiality (Lev. 20:16), female adulterers (Lev. 20:10), etc. In fact, we are not aware of any sin for which God kills guilty males but spares guilty females, except in the case of homosexual activity.

Is this a mistake? Is the Bible inconsistent? The answer, of course, is "No." The New Testament states that the Old Testament death penalties are just in the eyes of God. Hebrews 2:2 states that in the Mosaic Law, "...every transgression and disobedience received a just recompense...." The Bible prescribes death of the male homosexual and life for the female because only the male homosexual wastes seed. Which once again shows that wasting seed is an awful thing in the eyes of God.

Comparison Number Two:
Female/animal intercourse vs. female homosexuality

Leviticus 20:16
"16. If there is a woman who approaches any animal to mate with it, you shall kill the woman and the animal; they shall surely be put to death. Their blood-guiltiness is upon them."

Here we have another comparison of different sexual sins similar to the previous example. Women who mate with animals are to be killed, while women homosexuals are to be allowed to live. And what can account for the difference? Again we see that the only explanation of the above law is that the difference is in wasting seed. In female bestiality, the animal's seed is wasted. In female homosexuality, while sin is indeed committed, no seed is wasted.

So ends our examination of Old Testament perversions and their penalties. We may observe that all sterile sexual acts are forbidden, unless (as we have said) they happen accidentally. Therefore, since the very purpose of all methods of birth control is to make the sexual act sterile, they are forbidden too.

Comparison Number Three:
Male Homosexuality vs. Male Companionship and Sex Outside of Marriage.

Let us move into another area of comparison, and ask the question: "Exactly what is it about male homosexuality which makes it worthy of death?"

First, it can't be because of the mere fact that male homosexuals like to be in the company of men rather than women, for David said of Jonathan: "I am distressed for you, my brother Jonathan; you have been very pleasant to me. Your love to me was more wonderful than the love of women." (2 Samuel 1:26)

Second, the death penalty can't be because of the mere fact of men being physically affectionate to other men; for John says "There was reclining on Jesus' breast one of his disciples, whom Jesus loved." (John 13:23) And Paul says "Greet all the brethren with a holy kiss." (1 Thess. 5:26) (By the way, let us make it crystal clear that we repudiate the blasphemous suggestions of present and past homosexuals that Jesus and David were latent or active homosexuals. May such evil talk perish from the earth!)

Third, male homosexuals can't be executed because of the fact that sexual intercourse takes place outside the bonds of marriage, because according to the Bible there is no civil punishment for sexual relations between a single man and a single girl. (Deut. 22:28-29)

What then is left as a reason? Only this: male homosexuals are worthy of death because they emit semen outside the proper receptical contrary to nature as created by God. Thus they negate the purpose for which semen was created and "poured out" by God (Job 10:10): procreation. Birth control does the very same thing, and so is likewise under the curse of God.

REASON NUMBER SIX
CASTRATION AS A BLEMISH

(LEVITICUS 24:19-20, 21:17-20, 22:20-22,24-25

Deuteronomy 23:1, 25:11-12)

PART A. ANIMAL CASTRATION AS AN INJURY/BLEMISH

Leviticus 24:19-20
"19. And if a man INJURES his neighbor, just as he has done, so it shall be done to him: 20. fracture for fracture, eye for eye, tooth for tooth; just as he INJURED a man, so it shall be inflicted on him."

The Lord laid down a judicial principle for Israel in the above verses: every crime committed against a person was to be punished by an equal penalty against the criminal. It is not here our concern to explain the present day application of this particular set of verses -- suffice it to say that inflicting an "injury" on a fellow human being is clearly sinful. We intend rather to focus in on the word "injure", which occurs in both verses. The word in Hebrew is "mum," which means "blemish."

If you examine the various verses in which this word occurs, you will find that the Scripture contains listings of different types of blemishes. Here they are (with the English words translating "mum" being capitalized):

Leviticus 21:17-20
"17. Speak to Aaron, saying, 'No man of your offspring throughout their generations who has a DEFECT shall approach to offer the bread of his God. 18. 'For no one who has a DEFECT shall approach: a blind man, or a lame man, or he who has a disfigured face, or any deformed limb, 19. or a man who has a broken foot or broken hand, 20. or a hunchback or a dwarf, or one who has a defect in his eye or eczema or scabs or crushed testicles.'"

Leviticus 22:20-22, 24-25
"20. Whatever has a DEFECT, you shall not offer, for it will not be accepted for you. 21. And when a man offers a sacrifice of peace offerings to the Lord to fulfill a special vow, or for a freewill offering, of the herd or of the flock, it must be perfect to be accepted; there shall be no DEFECT in it. 22. Those that are blind or fractured or maimed or having a running sore or eczema or scabs, you shall not offer to the Lord, nor make of them an offering by fire on the altar to the Lord. 24. Also anything with its testicles bruised or crushed

or torn or cut, you shall not offer to the Lord, or do in your land, 25. nor shall you accept any such from the hand of a foreigner for offering as the food of your God; for their corruption is in them, they have a DEFECT. They shall not be accepted for you."

Note that in addition to blindness, crippledness, broken limbs, eczema and running sores, there also occurs bruised or crushed or torn or cut testicles! God here declares that damaged or destroyed testicles are a bad thing. We think that all would agree that the lists in the above verses are bad things; we have never seen anyone declaring the great benefits of being crippled or blind, or of having running sores! Once again, though, exceptions are made for birth control.

We are told in the news media and in sex manuals about the "quick and easy, virtually fool-proof method of birth-control -- vasectomy." Once again, what is a bad thing in Scripture is a "good thing" in our culture. But we Christians should seek to find out what the Bible says, not what the latest point of view is. And the Bible says that anyone who gets a vasectomy is injuring themselves, something forbidden by the Bible.

(As an aside, take a look at Lev. 22:24. This verse forbids offering defective animals to God, but according to a number of translators and interpreters of the Bible, it forbids the castration of animals as well. We see from numerous Bible passages that God cares about animals; some view Lev. 22:24 as a protective law for them. If this is the case, then we would say that if castration is forbidden for animals, it is certainly forbidden for people. But this point is not essential for our position; we throw it in because it is a possible argument against birth control.)

No matter what one thinks of the argument of the previous paragraph, he or she is still faced with the fact that the Scripture calls castration a blemish in animals. And if a destroyed or damaged reproductive system is a blemish for animals, how much more so for human beings, made in the image of God! Therefore neither permanent sterility (vasectomies) nor partial sterility (condoms) are permissable. Castration destroys the seed before it is made. Birth control destroys the seed after. It is only a matter of timing, and both do the same thing, namely, waste seed. (Tubal ligation, which is merely female castration, is by implication forbidden also.)

PART B. EUNUCHS IN ISRAEL

Deuteronomy 23:1
"1. No one who is emasculated, or has his male organ cut off, shall enter the

assembly of the Lord."

We see that the Scripture points to the badness of castration in Deu. 23:1. If a person who was a eunuch involuntarily was not allowed to be a full Israelite, what would God's view be towards someone who did this awful thing to himself because he wanted to prevent God from sending children into the world?

PART C. PUNISHMENT FOR POTENTIAL DAMAGE TO THE MALE REPRODUCTIVE SYSTEM

Deuteronomy 25:11-12
"11. If two men, a man and his countryman, are struggling together, and the wife of one comes near to deliver her husband from the hand of the one who is striking him, and puts out her hand and seizes his genitals, 12. then you shall cut off her hand; you shall not show pity."

This law is even more pointed than the previous one on eunuchs: in order that she may stop a man who is fighting with her husband, a lady grabs her husband's opponent by his sexual organs. What does God say to do with her? Do you reward her? Do you commend her for saving her husband? No. Rather, the civil authorities are commanded to take the lady and cut off her hand. They cannot cancel the punishment or change it. The lady gets her hand cut off whether she hurt the man or not.

We can observe that God is extremely angry with such a lady. If there is a fight and the woman grabs the man's hand or foot, she suffers no punishment, but if she grabs his sexual organs, she gets her hand cut off. God is, by these verses, showing that interfering with the sexual organs' job is strictly forbidden. And these verses become a proof text for forbidding birth control, because birth control prevents the sexual organs from carrying out their duties, just the same as grabbing the sexual organs in a fight has the potential to do. If God forbids the potential on pain of getting the hand cut off, how much more does God forbid the actual?

REASON NUMBER SEVEN

SEED AS SEMEN OR CHILDREN

(HEBREWS 7:9-10, JOB 10:8-11)

Hebrews 7:9-10
"9. And, so to speak, through Abraham even Levi, who received tithes, paid tithes, 10. for he was still in the loins of his father when Melchizedek met him."

Job 10:8-11
"8. Thy hands fashioned and made me altogether, and wouldst Thou now destroy me? 9. Remember now, that Thou hast made me as clay; and wouldst Thou turn me to dust again? 10. Didst Thou not pour me out like milk, and curdle me like cheese; 11. clothe me with skin and flesh, and knit me together with bones and sinews?"

If a person looks up the word "seed" in the Old Testament, an interesting fact will pop up. Namely, the Hebrew word "zerah" is used of human seed in two different ways: a) semen (as in Gen. 38:9 and Lev. 15:18,32), and b) children or people after birth (as in Gen. 46:6 and Lev. 22:13).

Some may say, "So what does that prove? The word 'house' can be used of a man's building or of a man's family. Likewise, just because the word for semen and offspring is the same word, this doesn't prove that they are the same thing."

To oppose this view we have reason and Scripture. The reason that Scripture uses the same word for semen and children is because all humans at one time existed is semen form. Without semen, no children are possible. So, viewing children as a continuous process, we can see that the word "seed" applies well to both stages of human life, before and after conception. Further, what is the reason that most methods of birth control seek to prevent the seed from uniting with a female egg? Is it not to prevent the birth of real people who may result from the semen produced by the sexual act? (Obviously, birth control does not seek to prevent the birth of imaginary babies! Imaginary babies do not need prevented!)

Next, the Scripture in Hebrews 7:1-10 proves the subservience of the Levitical priesthood to the prophesied Melchizedek priesthood of Christ by using the following logic: Levi is less than Abraham, and Abraham is less than Melchizedek -- therefore, the Melchizedek priesthood of Christ (prophesied by Psa. 110) is greater than the Levitical priesthood of the Mosaic Covenant.

During the argument of Hebrews, there occurs the following statement (7:9-10): "And, so to speak, through Abraham even Levi, who received tithes, paid tithes, for he was yet in the loins of his father when Melchizedek met him."

Note that Hebrews says that Levi, in some real (not imaginary) way, was in the loins of his great-grandfather (!) Abraham. Now, if Abraham had practised birth control and "succeeded", would he not have eliminated the real person Levi who was born some hundred years later, according to this verse?

Here is what John Owen said when commenting upon the Scripture, "for he was yet in the loins of his father when Melchisedec met him": "The force of this proof seems to depend on a double principle. 1. That children, the whole posterity of any one, are in his loins before they are born. And this principle is sure in the light of nature and common reason; they are in them as the effect in its cause; nor have they any future existence, but with relation unto their progenitors, even the remotest of them." (By the way, Owen was opposed to birth control, as may be observed from his comments upon Hebrews 13:4.)

Those who practise birth control should realize that what they are doing not only eliminates semen (which nobody seems to be concerned with), but thereby also eliminates future people. These eliminated people exist in the loins of those who practise birth control, and are subsequently destroyed by birth control.

We have encountered people who disagree with the above view because of what the Bible says about predestination. Such persons reason like this: "Well, God decides who will be born on earth. Therefore, if I practise birth control, and God gives me two children, that must be how many children God wants me to have. Therefore, since nothing can hinder God's mighty will, birth control is OK."

What shall we say to this? Well, we say that if this line of reasoning is correct, then nothing is a sin at all! For example, you could shoot your neighbor in the head and say, "Well, God could have stopped me from pulling the trigger, or he could have made the bullet miss. Therefore, since nothing can hinder God's mighty will, murder is OK." Or perhaps you might set houses on fire and say, "Well, since everything that happens is according to God's mighty will, then arson must be OK." Who is there among Christians who accepts such incredible sophistry when it comes to murder or arson? But -- many Christians swallow reasonings like this in order to justify conduct with which they already agree, like with Birth Control!

Of course, God has the ability to give couples children whether they practice Birth Control or not, but this proves nothing at all. According to Holy Scripture, God can make children out of rocks -- but if you are waiting for God to make kids for you this way, we think that you'll be waiting a long time. Those who use such reasonings to justify themselves need to realize that God has appointed godly means to accomplish godly ends. God wants to give us food, but he has willed that we should work to get it. Likewise, God wants to help us when we are in trouble, but he wants us to pray first. Now, God feeds lots of people who are lazy, and helps lots of people who don't pray as they should, but does this justify laziness or people who don't pray? Of course not! Likewise, God sometimes gives people children in spite of condoms, spermicides and withdrawal (and even abortion). This fact does not justify any of these unnatural activities! It is God's command that we have children, and therefore it is God's will that we have natural sexual intercourse to accomplish this goal.

Let us now examine God's Word concerning Sennacherib, the king of Assyria. (Isaiah 37:21-29) Sennacherib had invaded and destroyed Judah, as God himself had ordained long before the event (37:26). Yet does this fact of predestination show that Sennacherib's conduct was morally defensible? Absolutely not, as one may see from reading Isaiah 37:28-29. God was angry with Sennacherib for his ungodly conduct, even though God pre-ordained the event! This is, needless to say, a mysterious concept, but it should be apparent that predestination does not justify forbidden conduct. It is not without reason that Moses says in Deut. 29:29, "The secret things belong to the Lord our God, but the things revealed belong to us and to our sons forever, that we may observe all the words of this law."

As further proof that our view of birth control does not contradict the Biblical doctrine of predestination, we now quote from the writings of John Calvin, who, as we all know, surely believed in predestination:

"The voluntary spilling of semen outside of intercourse between man and woman is a monstrous thing. Deliberately to withdraw from coitus in order that semen may fall on the ground is doubly monstrous. For this is to extinguish the hope of the race and to kill before he is born the hoped-for offspring. This impiety is especially condemned, now by the Spirit through Moses' mouth, that Onan, as it were, by a violent abortion, no less cruelly than filthily cast upon the ground the offspring of his brother, torn from the maternal womb. Besides, in this way he tried, as far as he was able, to wipe out a part of the human race. If any woman ejects a foetus from her womb by drugs, it is reckoned a crime incapableof expiation and deservedly Onan incurred upon himself the same kind of punishment, infecting the earth by his semen, in

25

order that Tamar might not conceive a future human being as an inhabitant of the earth." (Calvin's Latin Commentary on Genesis -- 38:10)

Though Calvin certainly believed in predestination, yet he condemned birth control as the murder of future human beings. He certainly did not think that God's secret purposes justify conduct which the Word of God forbids.

As for our second Scripture passage, Job 10:8-11, we have included it because it is one of the few passages (if not the only one) in the Bible to describe the sexual act itself and relate it to the creation of an individual person. Verses 10 and 11 describe the emission of semen and its formation into a baby in the mother's womb. What is noteworthy about the verse is this: Job specifically says that it was him (Job) present in the semen of this father. Observe: "Didst thou not pour ME out like milk, and curdle ME like cheese?"

Having read anti-abortion literature published by Christians, we have noticed that a sizable portion of Bible texts cited to prove that children in the womb are human beings are passages like this: "Before I formed YOU in the womb I knew you, And before YOU were born I consecrated you...." (Jeremiah 1:5) Yet many who correctly oppose abortion also favor birth control, in spite of Job 10:10 which proves that human life is present in human semen. (If human life is not in human semen, then why do people use "spermicides", that is, "sperm killers"?) If it is wrong to destroy life in the womb, then it is wrong to deliberately kill semen.

Someone might say, "Oh, who is there in the Church who adopts such a ridiculous unscientific view of semen?" To which we would reply: "Martin Luther!" While commenting on Genesis 2:21, he said, "Thus it is a great miracle that a small seed is planted and that out of it grows a very tall oak. But because these are daily occurrences, they have become of little importance, like the very process of our procreation. Surely it is most worthy of wonder that a woman receives semen, that this semen becomes thick and, as Job elegantly said (Job 10:10), is congealed and then is given shape and nourished until the fetus is ready for breathing air." (Luther's Works, Vol. 1 pg. 126) By the way, Calvin agreed with Luther's view, as one may see by examining his comments upon the same verse.

Let us also take the time to point out that the Church of Christ should not get its moral standards from the pseudo-god of "modern science", but from the Holy Word of God, the Bible. The Bible and real science do not contradict each other at all, and where modern scientists draw erroneous conclusions from observations of the natural world, their conclusions are to be rejected. So, when "great medical authorities" declare that a baby in the womb is not to be regarded as a human being, we must toss their views into the trash. And we must do likewise with their views on birth control.

REASON NUMBER EIGHT
THE NATURAL FUNCTION OF WOMEN
(ROMANS 1:25-27)

Romans 1:25-27
"25. For they exchanged the truth of God for a lie, and worshiped and served the creature rather than the Creator, who is blessed forever. Amen. 26. For this reason God gave them over to degrading passions; for their women exchanged the natural function for that which is unnatural, 27. and in the same way also the men abandoned the natural function of the woman and burned in their desire towards one another, men with men committing indecent acts and receiving in their own persons the due penalty of their error."

God here says that cultures which reject the worship of God are punished by God "giving them over to degrading passions." The road to these degrading passions begins when men and women exchange "the natural function of women for that which is unnatural." This is stated in Romans 1:26-27. What is the ultimate result of rejecting the "natural function of women" ? -- homosexuality and other like perversions.

What is this "natural function" of women? Is it scrubbing the floor? Is it washing clothes? No, for men can do these things. The natural function of women is bearing children. All biological differences between men and women point to this conclusion. The physical differences between men and women are as follows:

1) Women menstruate; men don't
2) Women produce milk; men don't
3) Women have uteri; men don't
4) Men have male sexual organs; women don't

Note these differences. What are these differences for? So women can bear children. There is nothing else that can be described as the "natural function of women" other than childbearing. If you say that the natural function of women is sexual intercourse, not childbearing, then why do women have uteri, if they were not naturally to become pregnant? Why do women have breasts if not to feed babies? If childbearing is not the natural function of women, then why did God add all that "unnecessary" equipment which enables women to bear children? For it is readily apparent that breasts and uteri are unnecessary for a woman to engage in sexual intercourse.

It is evident that when God made woman, He did not add unnecessary parts. As Paul says in 1 Cor. 12:18, "...God has placed the members, each one of them, in the body, just as he desired." For what purpose did God give women uteri? So women could have intercourse? No, but rather that women could receive the seed from intercourse and nurture it. For what purpose did God give women breasts? So men could stare at them? No! Rather, so women could nurture the children which God gives to them. So it is apparent that sexual intercourse is but the means to accomplish the natural function of women, which is childbearing. And if this is true, then birth control is opposing the natural function of women.

Once again we quote from Martin Luther: "Moses numbers fertility among the blessings. 'There will not be a barren woman among you,' he says (cf. Ex. 23:26). We do not regard this so highly today. Although we like and desire it in cattle, yet in the human race there are few who regard a woman's fertility as a blessing. Indeed there are many who have an aversion for it and regard sterility as a special blessing. Surely this is also contrary to nature. Much less is it pious and saintly. For this affection has been implanted by God in man's nature, so that it desires its increase and multiplication. Accordingly, it is inhuman and godless to have a loathing for offspring." (Luther's Works, Vol. 5, p. 325)

REASON NUMBER NINE
CHILDBIRTH AND SALVATION FOR WOMEN

(1 TIMOTHY 2:11-15)

1 Timothy 2:13-15
"13. For it was Adam who was first created, and then Eve. 14. And it was not Adam who was deceived, but the woman being quite deceived, fell into transgression. 15. But women shall be saved through the bearing of children if they continue in faith and love and sanctity with self-restraint."

Here we have a "strange passage", according to most people today. "It can't mean spiritual salvation," say some.

If you look up the verses in Paul's letters which contain the word "saved" (the same one that is in vs. 15), you will find that every time Paul uses the word he is talking about spiritual salvation. Is Paul then saying that women can earn salvation by childbearing? By no means. Salvation cannot be earned or merited. Salvation is by grace and not by works.

What Paul is saying may be summarized as follows: If a woman is truly saved, she will prove her faith and her salvation by pursuing good works, which are (according to Jesus) inevitable for a true Christian. The pathway of teaching doctrine to husbands or ordering them around is not open to women. The pathway of obedience, which leads to eternal salvation, is (for married women) accompanied by childbearing if possible. Lest a woman think that the childbearing itself will save her, Paul adds that a woman bearing children will be saved if she continues in "faith and love and sanctity with self-restraint."

Paul's statement is paralleled by that of Jesus in Matthew 19:17, "If you wish to enter into life, keep the commandments." Christ says the same thing again in Luke 10:25-28. "And, behold, a certain lawyer stood up and put Jesus to the test, saying, 'Teacher, what shall I do to inherit eternal life?' And Jesus said to him, 'What is written in the Law? How does it read to you?' And he answered and said, 'You shall love the Lord your God with all your heart, and with all your soul, and with all your strength, and with all your mind; and your neighbor as yourself.' And Jesus said to him, 'You have answered correctly; do this, and you will live.'" Jesus is not preaching salvation by law or works. He is teaching that if a person is truly a Christian, good works will accompany him to eternal life. (It is not even possible to truly obey the law of God unless one is a Christian anyway.)

29

Paul is saying that the pathway to salvation for married women is attended by godly childbearing. Those who reject childbearing (when they are married) reject the good works which Paul says accompany salvation.

To demonstrate that we are not teaching "salvation by works," we will now quote Martin Luther and John Calvin, who unswervingly defended salvation by grace alone. Let us see what they say 1 Timothy 2:15 means.

Martin Luther on 1 Tim. 2:15: "15. 'SHE WILL BE SAVED.' That subjection of women and domination of men have not been taken away, have they? No. The penalty remains. The blame passed over. The pain and tribulation of childbearing continue. Those penalties will continue until judgment. So also the dominion of men and the subjection of women continue. You must endure them. You will also be saved if you have also subjected yourselves and bear your children with pain. 'THROUGH BEARING CHILDREN.' It is a very great comfort that a woman can be saved by bearing children, etc. That is, she has an honorable and salutary status in life if she keeps busy having children. We ought to recommend this passage to them, etc. She is described as 'saved' not for freedom, for license, but for bearing and rearing children. Is she not saved by faith? He goes on and explains himself: bearing children is a wholesome responsibility, but for believers. To bear children is acceptable to God. He does not merely say that bearing children saves: he adds: if the bearing takes place in faith and love, it is a Christian work, for 'to the pure all things are pure (Titus 1:15).' Also: 'All things work together,' Rom. 8:28. This is the comfort for married people in trouble: hardship and all things are salutory, for through them they are moved forward toward salvation and against adultery.... 'IN FAITH.' Paul had to add this, lest women think that they are good in the fact that they bear children. Simple childbearing does nothing, since the heathen also do this. But for Christian women their whole responsibility is salutary. So much the more salutary, then is bearing children. I add this, therefore, that they may not feel secure when they have no faith." (Luther's Works, Vol. 28, p. 279)

As for John Calvin, his comments on our Scripture passage are as follows: "15. BUT SHE SHALL BE SAVED. The weakness of the sex renders women more suspicious and timid, and the preceding statement might greatly terrify and alarm the strongest minds. For these reasons he modifies what he had said by adding a consolation....Paul, in order to comfort them and render their condition tolerable, informs them that they continue to enjoy the hope of salvation, though they suffer a temporal punishment. It is proper to observe that the good effect of this consolation is twofold. First, by the hope of salvation held out to them, they are prevented from falling into despair through alarm at the mention of their guilt. Secondly, they become accustomed to

30

endure calmly and patiently the necessity of servitude, so as to submit willingly to their husbands, when they are informed that this kind of obedience is both profitable to themselves and acceptable to God. If this passage be tortured, as Papists are wont to do, to support the righteousness of works, the answer is easy. The Apostle does not argue here about the cause of salvation, and therefore we cannot and must not infer from these words what works deserve; but they only shew in what way God conducts us to salvation, to which he has appointed us through his grace. THROUGH CHILD-BEARING. To censorious men it might appear absurd, for an Apostle of Christ not only to exhort women to give attention to the birth of offspring, but to press this work as religious and holy to such an extent as to represent it in the light of the means of procuring salvation....whatever hypocrites or wise men of the world may think of it, when a woman, considering to what she has been called, submits to the condition which God has assigned to her, and does not refuse to endure the pains, or rather the fearful anguish, of parturition, or anxiety about her offspring, or anything else that belongs to her duty, God values this obedience more highly than if, in some other manner, she made a great display of heroic virtues, while she refused to obey the calling of God. To this must be added, that no consolation could be more appropriate or more efficacious than to shew that the very means (so to speak) of procuring salvation are found in the punishment itself". (Calvin's Commentary, Vol. 21, p. 71)

CHAPTER TWO

TWO ALTERNATE VIEWPOINTS ON BIRTH CONTROL

by "A Concerned Friend"
and
Pastor Roger Kovaciny

and

THEIR REBUTTALS

by Charles D. Provan

The rest of the populace is more wicked than even the heathen them-selves. For most married people do not desire offspring. Indeed, they turn away from it and consider it better to live without children, because they are poor and do not have the means with which to support a household. But this is especially true of those who are devoted to idleness and laziness and shun the sweat and the toil of marriage. But the purpose of marriage is not to have pleasure and to be idle but to procreate and bring up children, to support a household. This, of course, is a huge burden full of great cares and toils. But you have been created by God to be a husband or a wife and that you may learn to bear these troubles. Those who have no love for children are swine, stocks, and logs unworthy of being called men or women; for they despise the blessing of God, the Creator and Author of marriage.

Martin Luther

ALTERNATE VIEWPOINT NUMBER ONE:

ANOTHER VIEW ON ONAN

By "A Concerned Friend"

What has been written on spilling the seed by Onan has been used to burden many, many consciences. Nobody has the right to burden the conscience wherein God does not burden it.

There is probably no married man, not even such as condemns the spilling of the seed most vehemently, who is not guilty of spilling the seed. Marriage is given not only for producing children, but also for the joy of sexual intercourse. Since this is so, every man who has intercourse with his wife during her infertile period is spilling the seed. Then in intercourse during the fertile period almost always ONLY ONE SPERMATOZOON penetrates the egg of the female. ALL THE REST, MILLIONS OF THEM, ARE SPILLED, WASTED. The Hebrew word used in Genesis 38 means to waste, corrupt, destroy, devastate. All but one are destroyed, wasted. Spilled, if you will. THEY DO NOT PRODUCE.

God himself destroys the seed - in regular intercourse, in night losses, in menstruation. All natural processes.

Onan is said to have been killed by God because he spilled the seed. THERE IS NOTHING IN THE WHOLE BIBLE THAT SPECIFICALLY CONDEMNS THE SPILLING OF THE SEED. BUT THERE IS SOMETHING IN THE BIBLE THAT SAYS THAT THE BROTHER OF A DEAD HUSBAND SHOULD GO INTO HIS WIDOW TO RAISE UP CHILDREN FOR THE DEAD - specifically the firstborn of the union. All kinds of sexual sins are condemned in the Word, but not once the spilling of the seed.

A brother could refuse to marry the dead brother's wife and not be killed for it. And so it is said the only difference between such an unwilling brother and Onan was that Onan spilled the seed and that therefore God killed him - IMMEDIATELY, according to Luther. There was another difference - a big difference. Onan did not refuse to marry Tamar, his brother's widow. If he had, Tamar, according to Deuteronomy 25: 5-10, could have taken off his shoe and spit into his face and thus shamed him. No, he married her. But he destroyed the seed during intercourse. Why? "Lest that he should give seed to his brother." THAT was his sin. To raise up seed for the brother was why Judah told Onan to marry Tamar, to go into her. We read: "And the thing which he did displeased the Lord: wherefore he slew him also." The Lord had slain Onan's wicked brother before that.

What was the "thing" that displeased the Lord? Onan did three things: 1. he spilled the seed; 2. he prevented birth; 3. he refused to give seed to his brother, although he married the widow. The whole idea was to raise up seed for his brother. Spilling the seed was only a means to that end, wicked end. It was like taking a vow and not fulfilling it.

It is a question whether God killed Onan immediately. The Hebrew verb used in Genesis 38:9 means in the tense used there (Piel): "Often, much, for a long time." It seems that God gave him time to repent of his refusal to give his brother seed. But Onan persisted. So God killed him.

The NIV and AAT both translate, not "when," but "whenever." So also other translators.

How can anybody say that spilling the seed is worse than adultery or even incest? Especially disturbing is this in view of the fact that nowhere in the Bible is spilling of the seed specifically forbidden! How can we condemn it if God himself spills the seed - in night losses, in intercourse, in menstruation?

It is said that wasting the seed is a violation of God's command to be fruitful and multiply. In the first place this is not an absolute command. Jesus did not marry. Paul did not marry. Many cannot marry even if they would. Secondly, God does not say anywhere that we must have as many children as possible. A person may be said to be fruitful even if he has only six children although having been capable of having many more.

God told our first parents to fill the earth. The earth is pretty well filled up. If all people from the beginning had had all the children they could possibly bear there would perhaps be no standing room on the earth.

It is said that God would supply the need of all the children brought into the world even if everybody produced as many children as possible, that a large family should not worry anybody. We know that God has blest richly many large families. But we all know families, large families, that cannot buy their food, that cannot pay their rent, that are suffering. They are families in our own churches.

Does this mean that Jesus failed to keep his promise in Matthew 6? No! If they are alive, the promise is being kept. He has his ways of providing.

Jesus may be testing the family. Or the family lacks faith or initiative. Paul was hungry at times. In Hebrews 11 we read of the martyrs, who at times were destitute. A destitute family may hesitate to add to an already suffering group.

If what Provan wrote is true, then nobody will be saved - outside of a handful of a handful. If any form of wasting the seed is sinful, then nobody will be saved - not any married folk. If any form of birth control is wrong, then perhaps a few people will be saved. I do not presume to advocate any form. But I don't want to judge those who use some forms of it, even if it involves wasting some seed. I believe it is a faulty exegesis to condemn all spilling of the seed on the basis of the Onan story. I repeat, EVERYBODY DOES IT IN SOME WAY OR OTHER. The seed is not human life. If it were, think of the millions of lives wasted in every intercourse.

I end as I began: Nobody has the right to burden consciences wherein God does not burden them.

A Concerned Friend

REBUTTAL NUMBER ONE:

REPLYING TO A CONCERNED FRIEND

ON THE SUBJECT OF ONAN

By Charles D. Provan

Since the *Christian News* of March 21, 1988, has printed a rebuttal to my article against birth control (CN of Feb. 29, '88), it is necessary for me to produce a "counter-rebuttal", so that the readers of CN may judge for themselves which position is Scriptural. Because our theological opponent on this issue has called himself "a concerned friend", we will call him this throughout our reply. When we use this term, we do not use it sarcastically, nor do we doubt his or her sincerity in attacking our position. Rather, we believe that our "concerned friend" is to be highly commended for his thinking about a subject which is very rarely considered by churchgoers today. For this, we are truly appreciative, for does not the road to changing one's mind on something begin by considering the subject first?

1.   Our friend begins his main argument by attempting to demonstrate that all emission of semen results in the death of the vast majority of the semen. It is of course true that each time sexual intercourse takes place, many individual sperm die, since only one sperm unites with the female egg. Many sperm die during nocturnal emissions. Therefore our concerned friend thinks that there is no difference between deliberate intentional destruction of semen and the death of semen which takes place during "non birth control" sexual intercourse.

However, this reasoning is not correct, because it leaves out the factor of the human will and intent. Concerning this subject, the Scripture is explicit -- this makes the difference between sin and non-sin in many cases.

For example, suppose a married woman is discovered engaging in sexual intercourse with a man who is not her own husband. What does the Bible say? The woman who engages in this act willingly is worthy of death. (Lev. 20:10) But if the woman is forced at gunpoint to do this thing, the woman goes free, without any blame being attached to her. (Deu. 22:25-27) In both cases, the act is the same. The only difference is the will of the female. This makes the difference between life and death. So it is with the death of the semen. If we have done our limited part to "be fruitful and multiply", it is enough. God does the rest, for, after all, it is God who creates children. But birth control involves intentional destruction of semen, the ultimate goal of which is to destroy the single semen which might combine with the female egg, conceiving a child.

To use another example: sometimes a woman who is pregnant will unintentionally do something which inadvertantly causes a spontaneous abortion, otherwise known as a miscarriage. (She may accidentally fall down the steps, for instance.) Do we attach moral blame to the woman? No. Rather, we sympathize with her misfortune. Yet if a woman goes to a doctor and pays him to exterminate her child while it is yet in the womb, we correctly say that she is a murderess. The results are exactly the same in both of our hypothetical cases, but how different are the acts in the eyes of God! Guilt is determined by the intent and action of the woman.

2.   According to our concerned friend, Onan was killed by God for refusing to give seed to his brother. Let us point out again that the man in Deuteronomy 25:7,9 also refuses to give seed to his brother. Yet this man is not killed. Therefore, the difference in conduct is the key to the difference in punishment, and the only difference in conduct is this: while both refused to give seed to his brother, only Onan destroyed his seed. Therefore, it is for this that he was killed by God. When we say this, we are not saying so on our own: we are saying it because careful consideration of the Scripture proves it, and in eighteen hundred years of church history, the view that Onan was killed because of his intentional destruction of semen is the universal view of the Christian Church. It is only in our "wonderful modern day churches" that birth control has become "approved". Let us be quick to point out that our century has also produced churches in abundance which have amazingly repudiated the infallibility of the Scriptures; churches which assert that abortion isn't murder, and homosexuality isn't a perversion! (We are by no means saying that those who disagree with us on birth control are in agreement with any of the preceding. We are merely pointing out that the same "bad tree" which produced the theological denial of Scripture and the theological acceptance of homosexuality and abortion also pushed for the acceptance of birth control.) We ask you, where did this view (that birth control is morally acceptable) originate? With those who believed the Bible, using it as their guide, or with non-believers? Any study of the modern birth control movement will show that it did not originate in the holy Church of God, but rather in pagans like Margaret Sanger.

Getting back to the statement of our friend that Onan's "spilling of seed" is no different than "spilling of seed" which occurs during "non birth control" sexual intercourse, we would also point out a fact which he has not commented upon. Namely, that out of all the verses which mention the emission of semen in the Old Testament, the Onan verse (Gen. 38:9, "he wasted his seed on the ground") is the only verse to employ the word "shachath" (which means "to waste, corrupt, destroy, devastate", as our friend has noted). This word is used in many passages as a synonym for "killed." (See, for example, Gen. 6:17, 9:15 and Judges 20:21) Do you think that there might be a reason for Onan's emission of seed to be described as a "killing" of seed, while all the other passages use words which merely mean "emit"? We do! In all other passages, no one does anything to intentionally harm the semen -- but in Onan's case, he deliberately killed his. If, as our concerned friend says, "There is nothing in the whole Bible that specifically condemns the spilling of the seed", then why does the Scripture use the very negative word "shachath" in Onan's case but not in any of the others?

3.   Another question raised by our friend is this: "How can anybody say that spilling the seed is worse than adultery or even incest?" Let me point out that Martin Luther said this, not me, but I think that his reasoning on the subject went something like this: "Adultery and incest, though great evils, at least perform the sexual act in a natural manner, allowing nature to take its course. Onan, on the other hand, took steps to frustrate God's creative activity, perverting nature. Onan's deed is an assault upon the natural order of things, and is therefore worse than adultery or incest." Luther may also have been influenced by the fact that although Tamar (Onan's wife) later committed incest with her father-in-law Judah (as Genesis 38 says), yet God did not kill her -- but he did kill Onan. We are not at this point able to positively affirm Luther's particular statement, as we wish to carefully consider the subject first. But, at the same time, neither do we wish to disagree with Dr. Luther, who certainly at the very least deserves our respect. So we will leave this particular statement on which sins are the worst (adultery and incest, or destroying one's semen) for later consideration. We emphatically do affirm, however, Luther's view on birth control: namely, that it is a great sin.

4.   Our friend also asks the question, "How can we condemn it [the spilling of seed] if God himself spills the seed - in night losses, in intercourse, in menstruation?" We agree that God does indeed do these things. Yet this does not mean that the intentional destruction of seed is permitted. By no means! We can easily prove that our friend's logic is incorrect, by examining parallel cases in the Bible. First, we shall examine the topic of miscarriages. The prophet Hosea says that God causes some miscarriages in order to punish people for sin: "Give them, O Lord -- what wilt Thou give? Give them a miscarrying womb and dry breasts." (Hosea 9:14) Does this mean that we humans are permitted by God to punish women by aborting their children? No, for Moses says that if a man causes an abortion, he shall be put to death. (Exo. 21:23). Likewise, God kills people all the time, as God declares in Deu.

32:39: "And there is no other god besides Me; It is I who put to death and give life." Because God, without moral blame, kills people all the time, does this mean that we can kill people when we please? Of course not, for God says to us, "You shall not murder." (Deu. 5:17) In the Bible, it is stated that God has killed children for the sins of their parents. For example, God said to Jeroboam I of Northern Israel: "You also have done more evil than all who were before you, and have gone and made for yourself other gods and molten images to provoke Me to anger, and have cast Me behind your back -- therefore behold, I am bringing calamity on the house of Jeroboam, and will cut off from Jeroboam every male person, both bound and free in Israel, and I will make a clean sweep of the house of Jeroboam, as one sweeps away dung until it is all gone." (1 Kings 14:9-10, fulfilled in 1 Kings 15:29) Yet God clearly forbids us from putting children to death for the sins of parents, as he says in Deu. 24:16: "Fathers shall not be put to death for their sons, nor shall sons be put to death for their fathers; everyone shall be put to death for his own sin." Scripture contains many things which are allowable to God but forbidden to us. So, just because God causes the vast majority of semen to die without causing the birth of a child, this does not prove that it is morally acceptable for us to cause semen to die by means of birth control.

5.   Later, our friend says that the command of God to be fruitful and multiply "is not an absolute command. Jesus did not marry. Paul did not marry. Many cannot marry even if they would." We would agree that the command to be fruitful and multiply is not an absolute command for all persons. We do not think that eunuchs, three year olds, women who are unmarried, and so forth, are obligated to do this, because they are not or cannot be married. The command is not an absolute command for all people, just married people. This is not unusual, for the command was not given to Adam until God had given him a wife, which makes sense to us! Is it not obvious that God's rules on divorce apply only to those folks who are married in the first place? God says that a husband should love his wife. Is this an absolute command of Gcd? Yes, but (obviously) it only applies to men who have a wife! Just because the command "be fruitful and multiply" does not apply to people who cannot or are not married, this by no means proves that it does not apply to those to whom the command was given, namely, married couples!

6.   Next, our theological opponent says, "God does not say anywhere that we must have as many children as possible. A person may be said to be fruitful even if he has only six children although having been capable of having more." Our reply is that, God does not need to say this directly for it to be so. He says it by implication. When God gave this command to Adam, to Noah's family and to Jacob, do you think God meant that they were to be fruitful for

only a day or a month or a year, or until they had a nuclear family? Or, as long as they were able? We think that the latter option is correct, since, if God had thought it was all right to limit God's blessings to the above people, he would have said so in the pertinent passages. Our friend's example of "six" being a good number of fruitfulness is to be faulted for the simple reason that, to us, being fruitful and multipying has no mandatory number. For Abraham and Sarah, their efforts to be fruitful produced only one child, Isaac. Even though they "multiplied themselves" by only one half (!), they had been doing their best to have children long before God himself made Isaac, and so they obeyed God to the extent of their ability. This is what God expects of us, not some particular number. What right do we have to cancel God's first blessing ("He blessed them," etc.; Gen. 1:28) to married couples?

7.   Our friend says, "God told our first parents to fill the earth. The earth is pretty well filled up, etc." I would ask, "How does he know this?" There are Christians and pagans who quite forcefully disagree with the idea that there is some sort of overpopulation crisis. (For example, R. J. Rushdoony in *The Myth of Overpopulation,* and Germaine Greer in *Sex and Destiny,* Chapter 14). In any case, let us look to Scripture for our guidance, not to the high priests of the new religions "Science" and "News Media". In Exodus 35:4-9, God told the Israelites to donate gifts to Moses to help build the tabernacle. When enough gifts were received to build it, God gave a revelation to Moses to tell the Israelites to stop giving. (Exo. 36:5-7) If God would give a revelation to stop, about something like this, don't you think that he would let us know when the world was full, to stop a command which has been in effect for some seven thousand years?! We could also ask the question, "If the world is full (so eliminating the command to be fruitful and multiply), then why does God still keep adding 'unnecessary' people to the 'already overpopulated' world?" After all, He is the one who causes children to be created, as Psa. 139:13 says: "For Thou didst form my inward parts; Thou didst weave me in my mother's womb." So this objection to our opposition holds no water.

8.   Our friendly opponent makes the overstatement, "The seed is not human life." Though we of course do not think that millions of little people die when someone has a nocturnal emission, nevertheless this statement needs to be qualified. The fact of the matter is that each seed is alive in a different sense than that of an ordinary cell in the human body: each seed is self-pro-pelled and can live even when separate from the body. No other types of cells in the human body have the ability to create new and separate human life, given the proper circumstances, except for the female egg, the female coun-terpart to the male seed. And if the seed is not "human life", then, pray tell, what type of life is it? Both myself and my opponent once existed as a seed, and I would call both him and myself human. If one eliminated all the human

semen from the earth, one would thereby eliminate all future humans also. So, there is a close connection between the two, so close that we do affirm that destroying semen is in effect destroying the children who would otherwise be born. And let it be plain to all, that those who practise birth control do so to eliminate children that they themselves do not wish to raise. They do not dislike the semen: they dislike the children the semen will turn into! In wartime, soldiers do not blow up trains becauses they don't like trains: they blow them up because they don't like what the trains deliver!

9.   It is of course true that "Nobody has the right to burden consciences wherein God does not burden them." We agree. But it is also true that we are commanded to "declare to My people their transgression." (Isa. 58:1) So, if birth control is a sin, then it is commendable and helpful to say so! Since the Bible says that it is a sin, and the holy Church of Christ has, since its inception, declared it to be so, we come to the conclusion that we are guilty of no sin in declaring that Christians should not practice birth control. And I can truthfully say that my motives are to strengthen the Church, not to tear it down.

If our opposition to birth control causes (humanly speaking) only one Christian family to have only one more beloved child of God, we consider our writings on the subject to be well worth the effort, and will praise God for the blessing!

Sincerely,

Charles D. Provan

ALTERNATE VIEWPOINT NUMBER TWO:

DEVIL'S ADVOCATE

By Rev. Roger Kovaciny

1.   Permit me to play the devil's advocate.

2.   (When a Roman Catholic is being considered for sainthood, the pope appoints a "Devil's Advocate." "Advocate" means "lawyer" and the devil's advocate is supposed to dig up all the dirt on the proposed saint. His job is to find reasons against the sainthood even though he may personally favor it.)

3.   I'm not attacking February 29's front-page article "The Bible's View of Birth Control" but somewhere in this journal the questions this article raised should be answered.

4.   Nor do I have a vested interest in birth control. Since we got married, my wife has had a baby every year or two. Our youngest died ten weeks ago, and the best news anyone could give us now is that the Lord is sending someone to fill the hole in our hearts. But somebody has to ask the questions that Charles Provan did not answer.

5.   First, the command to "be fruitful and multiply" is only HALF the commandment. It is half of a BALANCED commandment. The other half is, "...to fill the earth AND SUBDUE IT."

6.   Most people and nations seem to get either one half or the other way out of proportion. Western nations are committing race suicide because they are so interested in bringing the earth into subjection -- that is to say, having things the way they want them in their environment by the purchase of goods, services and machinery -- that they refuse to have enough children to even replace themselves, much less fill the earth.

7.   In the Third World, however, some parents have children that have to be put out in the street to steal or starve at the age of three because the parents are so busy filling the earth that they can't "subdue the earth" sufficiently to keep body and soul together.

8.   Further, the article fails to answer the question of why people today don't want children. A chief reason why people today do not regard children as a blessing is the radical restructuring of society that happened after the

Industrial Revolution. Two hundred years ago, a young man asked Franklin what was the quickest way to get rich. Franklin said, "Marry a widow with nine children." That was true then, when children as young as three were productive members of the family. Their labor may have been worth only a dime a day, but if their room and board only cost a nickel, they were productive, because a nickel was an important part of the family's income.

9.   But the same advice would bankrupt a man today, because today children are not able to be productive members of society. Jobs today pay a lot more but they are too complicated to learn until the teens or twenties. Meanwhile, children are an unremitting expense.

10.   What concerns me about Provan's article is the failure to recognize these facts and the failure to see how the changing structure of society changes the applicability of various Scriptures. For instance, the blessing of a large family was immediately evident in the days when the family was your main form of old-age insurance. Now that we have Social Security, we depend on other people's children instead of our own. The church has to consider such facts before making doctrinal pronouncements.

11.   And the Scripture that must be considered when doing this is contained in Matthew 23:4, where Jesus pronounced seven woes upon the Pharisees. One of their faults was that "They tie up heavy loads and put them on men's shoulders, but they themselves are not willing to lift a finger to move them."

12.   We should recognize that every child is a burden, even though a very precious one -- we would give our health, our comfort, and everything we own to have "little sister" back. But the church also has to deal with birth control evangelically, rather than legalistically. In other words, we have to make people want children by helping them raise them, instead of demanding that they shoulder the burden out of a sense of duty.

13.   We cannot assume that shouldering these burdens will automatically bring about the blessings needed to bear the load. In the first place, we may be misunderstanding the Bible. In the second place, we have the experience of others to warn us. Look at Utah, where the Mormons frown on birth control and encourage early marriage and large families. Utah has one of the highest divorce rates in the country, at least partly because of the great strain put on a marriage by having many children. So if we load heavy burdens on backs, at the very least we have to lift a finger to help them.

14.   This is what Lutherans do in our crisis-pregnancy counseling, isn't it? Unlike the evangelicals and fundamentalists, whose approach started out as a legislative one and only lately has become one of helping the unwed mother with the burdens caused by an unplanned child, our approach from the very first was to offer help to the hurting so that unwilling mothers could cope with the various burdens a child brought about. We cannot deny that there is hardly a surer road to poverty in this country than being a single mother, and as we try to deal with that issue, we also must deal with the fact that the birth of each child usually brings a lot more stress into a family than there was before.

15.   Now are we as a church "lifting a finger" to the strains of our brothers and sisters in Christ? For instance, are those who choose to be DINC's (DINC means "Double income, no children") until their mid-thirties recognizing that they have so much more disposable income that they should consider double-tithing both salaries to take some of the burden of supporting the church off large families? Do they think of families with many children when they decide to discard something, like for instance an old car, that is still good but which they are tired of? Do they give heavily of their time to the church to take some of the burden off parents? This year someone we know only as "Santa's Helper" gave each of our children a new pair of winter boots, and a toy. We still haven't the faintest idea who "Santa's Helper" is. I would like to think he, she, or they are childless adults helping out the largest family in the parish, not just parishioners helping out the pastor's family after a Christmastime death. Maybe they are both.

16.   Since the structure of society provides a great many of the reasons why people, even Christians, sometimes consider sterility a good thing, the Christian citizen can be doing what he thinks best to change the structure of society.

17.   For instance, in my opinion the replacement of Social Security with compulsory private insurance would do a lot toward bringing child-bearing back into fashion. Wage-earners should still have old-age taxes taken out of their checks, but those funds should be used to buy I.R.A.'s from private agencies. The government should have nothing to do with it. In this way, at least, people wouldn't be depending on everybody else's children to support them. And since they would own the proceeds, instead of it disappearing on their deaths, the IRA's would become part of their estate -- they might want to have somebody to leave it to.

18.   In Provan's account of Onan, which was very thoughtfully done, we must still answer this question: whether there is a further reason explaining

the bare words of Scripture. "Because he wasted his seed" is the stated reason. But by practicing coitus interruptus, Onan was doing more. He did what Ananias and Sapphira did in the sixth chapter of Acts: taking what he wanted, having the appearance of respectability and the pleasure of inter-course, while fraudulently depriving his dead brother's wife of what she wanted, the completion of intercourse and the blessing of children to support her in her old age and to carry on the name of her dead husband.

19.   Next, Provan quotes Calvin, but doesn't fully understand him.

20.   When Calvin said, "Onan, as it were by a violent abortion, no less cruelly than filthily cast upon the ground the offspring of his brother," we have to understand that Calvin believed in the medieval Garden Theory of Repro-duction. Human conception was not properly understood in the Middle Ages.

21.   The theory in vogue in Calvin's time was that (to put things in modern terms) the man did not provide merely the sperm. He provided the zygote, in other words the whole baby -- not just half its genes. Thus Calvin thought that the baby was not "conceived" but "implanted." The baby therefore got nothing from its mother except a "garden" to grow in -- one medieval medical book taught that the baby was already fully formed, although microscopic, from the instant when it left its father's loins. This is why Calvin regarded coitus inter-ruptus as tantamount to abortion. Moses, however, did not teach this. Moses wrote by inspiration and therefore did not make scientific mistakes.

22.   There is one further scientific misunderstanding in the article. On page 13, column 3 first paragraph, it is contended that menstruous inter-course cannot produce children. There's a word for people who believe that. They're called, "Parents." And that fact does change the conclusions of the section "Reason No. 5."

23.   The auther does not prove his point about the neutering of animals. The passage he quotes only speaks of animals that were to be used as offerings. Good thing, too; if we could not neuter dogs and cats, the world would be overrun with them and the only alternatives we would be left with would be the constant vigilance of sexual segregation and the annual de-struction of enormous numbers of our pets. Kill a puppy sometime and see if you think that is more humane than minor surgery.

24.   And yet another medical and theological overstatement: in column 4 on page 13, it says "Tubal ligation, which is merely female castration, is by implication forbidden also." Tubal ligation is merely female vasectomy. Fe-male castration is rather ovariectomy. Nor can we make doctrines "by impli-

cation"; otherwise "by implication" we would conclude what the author denies, that lesbians were to be executed as well as queer men.

25.　　And I wouldn't be as positive as he is, that they weren't. It's just that lesbianism would be much less common then, and less mentioned. Why? We have to take into account the tremendous value placed upon having children in ancient times. In fact, the main religions of the Holy Land were fertility cults, intended to improve the fertility of men's flocks, their fields, and their wives. Remember that to primitive people, the major sources of wealth are fields, flocks, and the children needed to work them. It should also be remembered that among the ancient Greeks, who practiced recreational sex, homosexuality was almost preferred but the homos still put up with having wives for the purpose of bearing children. Children were that highly valued.

26.　　Once again, I write merely as the devil's advocate. I am not now disagreeing or agreeing with the author's thesis, just pointing out as a friendly critic the questions that have to be answered before this issue is presented as a dead certainty to the church. The writer did a good job of presenting his case. Perhaps he is as well qualified as anyone to answer these questions and finish the job.

REBUTTAL NUMBER TWO:

REPLYING TO THE DEVIL'S ADVOCATE

By Charles D. Provan

So that our readers may better follow our answers to Pastor Kovaciny's "Devil's Advocate", we will proceed in the same order as his paragraphs.

Our comments upon:

Paragraph 3   It is of course legitimate to bring up questions about our views upon birth control. The Apostle Paul himself brings up questions some would ask about salvation, and Peter says that we should not fear questioning of our faith.

Par. 6   It is true that the nations of the West are committing race suicide. This is because they deserve it. We wish we could say otherwise. As the Scripture says, "The posterity of the wicked will be cut off." (Psalm 37:38) Because of our culture's desertion of God and his Christ, we are in a period of sad decline, brought about by our own wickedness.

Par. 7   While it may be true that in the Third World some parents sell their children, yet we may also observe that Scripture says, "I have been young, and now I am old; yet I have not seen the righteous forsaken, or his descendants begging bread." (Psalm 37:25) It also says, "But seek first His kingdom and His righteousness; and all these things [food and clothing; C.P.] shall be added unto you." (Matthew 6:33)

But if, in accordance with his secret plan, God would cause a great catastophe, which would affect the children of believers in a negative way, we may be assured that God has some reason for it, as in the case of Job's children (Job 1:18-19) or Joseph's slavery (Genesis 37, 39-40, 50:20). These emergencies do not justify wasting seed; for in the case of a temporary great catastrophe, we ought to listen to the word of the Apostle Paul, who said during a crisis at Corinth (1 Cor. 7:26), "those who have wives should live as if they had none." (1 Cor. 7:29) That is, couples ought to have no sexual relations at all. Note, he does not say that "due to the present crisis, I want Christian couples to practice withdrawal or other unnatural non-procreative practices." Likewise, when God told Jeremiah not to have children in Palestine due to the upcoming invasion by the Babylonian army, he instructed him not to get married; which makes no sense if God allows deliberately non-procreative sex in marriage. So that Christian couples do not classify every bad circumstance as a "crisis" justifying no sexual activity, please note what God told the Israelites who were slaves in Babylon: "This is what the LORD Almighty, the God of Israel, says to all those I carried into exile from Jerusalem to Babylon: ...'Marry and have sons and daughters; find wives for your sons and give your daughters in marriage, so that they too may have sons and daughters. Increase in number there; do not decrease.'" (Jer. 29:4,6) Note also that when the Israelites were in great bondage in Egypt, it was still God's will for them to be fruitful and multiply, as Moses says in Exo. 1:7,12,20. (We say this so that present day Christians do not use the "crisis" of not being able to vacation in Acapulco as an excuse for not having more children for God!)

Par. 8   D.A. says that up until approximately 200 years ago, (with the coming of the Industrial Revolution) people wanted children because they were a monetary asset. But in saying this he is not aware of several historical facts which disprove his point.

For example, Egyptian contraceptive "medicines" are mentioned as early as 1900 B.C.! Jewish records also speak of effective methods of birth control, utilizing available chemicals. Socrates, a well known philosopher, mentioned that population should be kept down to prevent countries from falling "into poverty or war". Another famous philosopher, Aristotle, mentioned various methods of preventing conception without objection. (And why would he object, since he was in favor of abortion as a means of population control?) The Cretans desired low-level populations, and encouraged homosexuality to accomplish this. The Greeks and Romans practiced exposure of infants. Caesar Augustus promulgated legislation to push people into having children, but his attempt failed: the historian Tacitus says "childlessness prevailed". The Carthaginians and Canaanites practiced unnatural sex and child sacrifices -- practices which obviously lowered the population. Pliny the Younger (c 100 A.D.) says that he lived "in an age when even one child is thought a burden preventing the rewards of childlessness".

Against this atmosphere of anti-children ideas and practices the early Church took its stand opposing contraception. (To list all the Church fathers would take up too much space.) The non-Christian populations of the Empire still practiced birth control, viewing children as a burden, as is evidenced by the heated condemnation of birth control by Jerome, Chrysostom, Ambrose, Augustine and many more.

I do know not much about society's view of children after the fifth century A.D., but I do know that the Catholic Church was continually fighting against birth control, which seems odd if "children were greatly desired before the Industrial Revolution." In the 1500's Martin Luther wrote, "Today you find many people who do not want to have children" (LW Vol. 1 p. 118). (Note that he said this some 250 years prior to 1800 and D.A.'s start of the Industrial Revolution!) Luther went on to state that the main reason for people's reluctance to have children was economic -- the same as it is today. In addition, an eminent Puritan named Richard Stock (d. 1626) said, "Again, in the use of marriages; many men and women, though they desire some children, not many...." (Stock opposed birth control, too.)

Par. 9   D.A. says that having lots of children "would bankrupt a man today". He says that "children are an unremitting expense". I would ask, "From where does D.A. get his view? From the Bible, or from the wisdom of the world? Does not marriage cost a lot? Does this prove that marriage is no longer a duty for those without continence?"

Par. 10   Our Devil's Advocate states: "What concerns me about Provan's article is the failure to recognize these facts and the failure to see how the changing structure of society changes the applicability of various Scriptures".

First, where does D.A. get his proof that "the changing structure of society changes the applicability of various Scriptures". He says that in the old days many children were valued as old-age insurance, but now that Social Security is here (!) the church should reconsider its opposition to B.C. Where does Scripture allow for reasonings which transform the clear teachings of the Bible into their opposites? Let us listen to what the Word of God says in Isaiah 5:20: "Woe to those who call evil good and good evil, who put darkness for light and light for darkness, who put bitter for sweet and sweet for bitter." Does not this apply to D.A.'s statements? He says many children (a great blessing in Psa. 127) is now a "burden" which will result in financial destruction; on the other hand, he has nothing bad to say for couples who deliberately make themselves childless, which the Bible consistently calls a great calamity!

Where in Scripture is it stated that "changing society" changes the moral precepts of God? Should it not rather be the moral precepts of God which change society? And if D.A.'s method of interpreting Scripture is acceptable, what well-respected theologian is there to back his view for the first four centuries of Protestantism?

Par. 11   D.A. says that people who condemn birth control may themselves be in danger of the condemnation of Jesus (Mt. 23:4)! I would again ask whether D.A. views the entire church for its first 19 centuries as under the condemnation of God? Logically they would have to be, because the Christian church has always opposed B.C., until one reaches the corrupt and decrepit twentieth century. Let D.A. be aware that his argument is used today by many who would change the rules which the church has held for 2000 years. We are told for example, that the church has been opposed to women preachers because of male chauvinism. Now, however, in our "enlightened" society, when we realize that this is "sexism", we should change the rules of the church instituted by Paul himself. Nowadays we are also informed that the church's 2000 year teachings on Scripture and homosexuality are just cultural, and so should be changed. This type of thought leads the Church to shipwreck the faith. (By the way, I am not saying that D.A. is pro-women elders, pro-homosexuality or anti-scripture. I am saying that his approach to Scripture interpretation ("change society/change application of Scripture") is very dangerous and is a major support of the enemies of the Church, as well as some of its misguided friends.)

Par. 12   We do not agree. Where does Scripture call children a burden? Scripture rather calls children a blessing and a great responsibility in so many passages we couldn't list them all here. We are not dealing with B.C. "legalistically", for legalism is demanding that people follow non-Scriptural rules (such as hand washing in Matthew 15). Since our opposition to B.C. is based squarely on Scriptural principles, we are not behaving legalistically, but Scripturally. Since this is so, let us apply some other words of Jesus to those who have many children out of obedience to God's command: "Take my yoke upon you, for it is light". (Mt.11:30) The burdens of the Pharisees were heavy because they were stupid, oppressive and unscriptural.

D.A. says that "we have to make people want children by helping them to raise them, instead of demanding that they shoulder the burden out of a sense of duty". Is this Scriptural? Should we not love God because it is a command? Of course, for Scripture says "Jesus replied; 'Love the Lord your God with all your heart and with all your soul and with all your mind. This is the first and greatest commandment.'" (Matt. 22:37-38) Should we not also want to love God? Of course: "We love because he first loved us." (1 John 4:19) I love my wife because Scripture commands me to do so and also because I want to, out of gratitude for her kindness to me. So what's wrong with having children because: a) God says it is my duty, and b) they are a great blessing? Children obey parents because they want to please their parents AND because they'll get paddled if they don't!

Par. 13   It is stated by D.A. that "We cannot assume that shouldering these burdens [having children; C.P.] will automatically bring about the blessings needed to bear the load." To which we say, "Why not?" After all, doesn't Jesus say, "But seek first his kingdom and his righteousness, and all these things will be given to you as well." (Mat. 6:33) So if a godly couple seeks to obey God by being fruitful, why shouldn't they (in a godly manner) expect God to help them? Jesus also said, "Look at the birds of the air; they do not sow or reap or store away in barns, and yet your heavenly Father feeds them. Are you not much more valuable than they?" (Mat. 6:26) We would say that this great promise of Jesus applies not only to believers, but also to their children.

D.A.'s example of "life in Utah" doesn't prove anything because: 1) Mormons aren't exactly "orthodox Christians", and 2) our culture encourages easy divorce, wifely rebellion and material dissatisfaction. Is it not reasonable that our evil culture would be in effect in Utah? As responsibilities increase, the ungodly will take the easy way out. But the Christian is not permitted to do so. "Enter through the narrow gate, for wide is the gate and broad is the road that leads to destruction, and many enter through it." (Matt. 7:13) And of course, if I am in favor of people not practicing B.C., then it is the duty of myself and other Christians to help out with more than words: "Let us not love with words or tongue but with actions and in truth." (1 John 3:18)

Par. 14   Let no one say that we are in favor of illegitimate children simply because we oppose B.C. Rather, we are in favor of abstinence before marriage, and are in favor of natural sexual relations during marriage.

Par. 15   We are opposed to "DINC"ism. No Christian has the right to choose "DINC", though it may come to some without their having anything to do with it. Is it right for married women to desire something which Scripture calls a shame and a reproach?

Par. 16   Knowing "why people, even Christians, sometimes consider sterility a good thing" does not affect the teaching of God. It is Scripture which counts, and it says that sterility is bad, so bad that it is described as sickness (Gen. 20:17-18), a disgrace (Luke 1:25), a curse (Hosea 9:11) and a cause of great misery and bitterness (1 Sam 1:10,11 and Gen. 30:1).

Par. 17   Of course we would agree that Social Security should be replaced by responsible Christian stewardship. The government should encourage people to have godly children; as the Scripture says: "A large population is a king's glory, but without subjects a prince is ruined." (Prov. 14:28) Isn't this happening to the once great but now dying United States?

Par. 18   Far be it from us to say that Onan wasn't selfish or greedy, for we think that he was all that. But it is Scripture which focuses in on Onan's destruction of semen as the cause of his death. As Gen. 38:10 says, "WHAT

HE DID was wicked in the Lord's sight; so he put him to death also." The Church has always taught that willful destruction of semen is an awful deed.

Let us look at the death of Ananias and Sapphira in Acts. Peter specifically says that they were killed by God because they lied to the Holy Spirit. But who would deny that lying and being greedy are sins to be condemned on the basis of the same story? In the same way, the Scripture says that Onan was killed by God for what he did, and what he did was kill his semen. So we would say that this is the primary point of the Onan incident; yet we would agree that the Onan story can be used to condemn greed and theft. The opponents of birth control are not faced with an either/or situation in the matter of Onan, for Scripture still condemns Onan specifically for destroying his seed. It is those who favor birth control who must come up with all kinds of absurd reasons to totally exclude destruction of semen as the reason (or even "a" reason) for Onan's death. The burden of proof is entirely upon them, not us.

D.A. says that Onan "deprived his dead brother's wife of what she wanted." Of course, we would agree with this part of D.A.'s assertion, and move on to an even more important question; namely "What is it that God himself wants from married couples?" Is it not, "Be fruitful and multiply"? (Gen. 1:28 NASV)

The Augsburg Confession says that Genesis 1:28 proves that "God created men for procreation" (Augsburg Confession Section 23, on "The Marriage of Priests.") The Westminster Confession alludes to the same verse when it says that marriage was instituted by God "for the increase of mankind with a legitimate issue and of the Church with a holy seed." The Confession quotes Mal. 2:15 (which speaks of marriage) as proof of this doctrine. It says, "Has not the Lord made them one? In flesh and spirit they are his. And why one? Because he was seeking godly offspring." And is not B.C. intended to thwart the goal of the sex act, the creation of children? The facts are these: a) according to the Bible, God creates, nurtures and causes children to be born, and b) people are not pleased with God's plan, so they practise B.C. to prevent God from sending them more children. (Isn't this perfectly obvious?)

Listen to God's word in Ezekiel 16:21: "You slaughtered my children and sacrificed them to idols." Again in Ezekiel 23:37, God says, "they even sacrificed their children, whom they bore to me..." God here condemns the Israelites for killing his children. Children of believers are here called "my children" by God. And by birth control we prevent God (insofar as it lies with us) from sending more of his children into the world, children which would otherwise be conceived and nurtured according to the mighty power of God.

Thus, as the Pharisees of old, we nullify the commands of God by our traditions. (Mat. 15:3)

Par. 20   The problem is not that I don't understand Calvin, because he is quite easy to understand. The "problem" is really for D.A. to convince us that Calvin is in error when he viewed birth control as murder and abortion! For, if Calvin is correct, then the churches of today are filled to the brim with unrepentant murderers and abortionists. What does D.A. offer to prove that Calvin believed in the "garden theory of reproduction"?: Nothing. Further, if Calvin did believe in the garden theory, then why does he say that Onan, by wasting his seed, "tried, as far as he was able, to wipe out a part of the human race." If the garden theory is true, Calvin had no need to add this phrase to his exegesis; he would have said, "Onan actually did wipe out a part of the human race, since there are little fully formed people in the seed." Lastly, even if Calvin did believe the garden theory, what does that prove? Calvin does not say "And we know Onan was bad because of the garden theory" -- he does not even mention it!

In what way does "modern science" refute Calvin's view of Onan? Modern science certainly agrees that the human sperm is a cell unlike any other cell - it is alive in and of itself, and it moves by itself. And, killing the sperm kills the life which (according to Job 10:10) God forms into people. Abortion, infanticide and B.C. are all just tools to eliminate children who people don't want, in defiance of God's revealed will. If people weren't worried about God sending unwanted children their way, why would they practice B.C. in the first place? After all, you don't need to prevent what cannot possibly happen!

At this time we would like to point out a weak spot in our opponent's armor: namely, his reliance upon the ethical conclusions of "modern science" when it comes to Birth Control. Our view is that the Holy Scriptures are to be our source for theology. The Church should not reject the seven day creation because of what pagan geology professors say about rock formations. We should not get our views on predestination from scientific atom particle diffusion patterns, which supposedly disprove predestination. And likewise, we should not get our views on Birth Control from genetic engineering and eugenic researchers. Our views as Christians should come from the Bible. When you want some poison gas or a neutron bomb, see a scientist; when you want to know if using these weapons is morally defensible, consult the Bible. Let us not forget that the greatest "scientific achievement" of this century was the development of the atomic bomb -- a great moral accomplishment for post-Christian man!

Par 21   Our friend asserts that Calvin believed in "implantation", not "conception", but if one looks at Calvin's statement, he says, "in order that Tamar might not CONCEIVE a future human being." Please note that the foregoing capitalized word in Calvin's original Latin is "conciperet", which means "conceive" (as in conception!).

Also, please note the great importance which Scripture applies to the semen: Levi was in Abraham's loins (Heb. 7:10); Christ was in David's loins (Acts 2:30, 2 Sam. 7:12); the genealogies in the Old Testament and the New are reckoned by the men, not women (Matt. 1, Luke 3, Gen. 11:10-26, Ezr. 2:61-62); We all died through Adam, not Eve! (Romans 5:17); Life comes from the semen (Job 10:11).

Par. 22   D.A. says that we are wrong because we say that "menstruous intercourse cannot produce children". (Our original article in *Christian News* erroneously stated that menstrual intercourse was sterile; we have corrected this oversight in this edition.) He says that "this fact does change the conclusions of the section 'Reason #5'" But, as a matter of fact, it doesn't change our conclusions at all, for we specifically allowed for minor exceptions. We said in our paper that "Withdrawal is meant to be sterile, and is, most of the time." (See Reason #5 of Chapter One of this book) We admit that it is possible to become pregnant by sex during menstruation, but only just possible, the same way it is possible to become pregnant by the method of withdrawal. Nonetheless it is in fact practically sterile, as was apparent some 2000 years ago (the Jewish philosopher, Philo of Alexandria, refers to this fact, now verified by observation). For further information, see page 33 of Pregnancy, Birth and Family Planning, by Alan F. Guttmacher, M.D.

Par 23   D.A. is correct in saying that we did not prove our point about Scripture forbidding castration of animals. (Our original Birth Control article in *Christian News* stated this: "Take a look at Lev. 22:24. This verse forbids offering defective animals to God, but it says more than that -- it forbids the castration of animals. We see from numerous Bible passages that God cares about animals; this is a protective law for them.") Because of insufficient evidence, we have "softened" our original paragraph into the paragraph now present in our booklet (paragraph 5 of Reason Number Six).

In any case, this does not destroy our point, for castration is still called a blemish for animals, and is therefore still a blemish for humans. (Unless we wish to say that blindness and being crippled are not blemishes for humans, though they are for animals!)

Par. 24   D.A.'s restricted definition of castration is technically correct. We, however, were using "castration" in its wider definition, which is: "to emasculate, to geld, to deprive of virility or procreative power." Since tubal ligation certainly does "deprive the female reproductive system of procreative power", in mostly the same way a vasectomy "does deprive the male reproductive system of procreative power", we feel justified in referring to both as castration.

D.A. says "Nor can we make doctrines 'by implication'". But on the contrary, many times Scripture proves things "by implication". For just a few examples: 1) David's eating of shewbread (1 Sam. 21:1-6) proves that healing is OK on the Sabbath (Mark 2:23-28); 2) God's care for oxen treading grain (Deut. 25:4) proves that ministers should be paid (1 Tim 5:17-18); 3) The Israelites gathering enough manna proves that Christians should share (Exo. 16:18, 1 Cor. 8:13-15); 4) The birds getting grain proves that God is concerned with us. (Mat. 6:26); 5) Evil men doing good things proves that God is even more good toward us (Mat. 7:11, Luke 18:1-8); 6) Women shouldn't be elders, proven by Eve's being decieved by the Devil (1 Tim 2:12-14).

And so, since proving things by implication is a Scriptural method of interpreting and applying Scripture, we feel entirely justified in reasoning that "since castration or damaging of the male reproductive organs is described in very negative terms, it thereby follows that castration or damaging of the female reproductive organs is also viewed by God in a very negative way. Since this is so, women are not allowed to get tubal ligations."

Par 24 & 25   Concerning lesbianism, I reject as unproven his "by implication" statement that lesbianism is worthy of the civil death penalty. Lesbianism, though evil, is nowhere ascribed a death penalty in any Jewish or Christian source that I am aware of. D.A. says (without proof) that Lesbianism was "much less common." To us, it would seem that in a culture where men were openly homosexual, that women, partly out of reaction, would turn to themselves or their own sex - After all, once the natural order of God is given up, there's nowhere to go but downhill.

Par 25   D.A. mentions the "great desire of ancient people for children", a statement which he does not prove. I am aware of many cultures which viewed children with disdain. While it is true that the nations which surrounded Israel had religions which are called, "fertility cults", yet is also true that these cultures mainly valued fertility of crops and animals, not children. In fact, one of the most powerful methods of "worshipping" the fertility gods, such as Molech and Chemosh, was by child sacrifice and non-procreative sex! These things were done, not to increase the number of children, but to ensure peace and food.

It would also be enlightening to look at Greece, which D.A. says "highly valued" children. Plato, one of the greatest of the Greek philosophers, was in favor of laws which would prohibit childbearing after the first ten years of marriage; he was also in favor of what we would call "zero population growth." As we have stated earlier, his disciple Aristotle thought abortion was OK. We know of only a few pagan Greeks expressing "pro-children" views. They were ignored, so much so that about 150 B.C. the Greek general Polybius said, "In our time all Greece was visited by a dearth of children....and a failure of productiveness followed....by our men's becoming perverted to a passion for show and money and the pleasure of an idle life and accordingly either not marrying at all, or, if they did marry, refusing to rear children that were born, or at most one or two out of a great number for the sake of leaving them well off or bringing them up in extravagant luxury."

Does this ancient Greek attitude toward children sound familiar? It should, for this same mindset is rotting the core of Western and Eastern Europe, as well as the United States, the areas which once were the bastions of Christianity.

CONCLUSION

We believe that the questions and statements of our "Devil's Advocate" do not negate the Bible's opposition to Birth Control. We hope that many of our readers (including Pastor Kovaciny!) would come to agree, thereby causing them to receive with joy many more gifts from God.

In closing, we would like to thank Pastor Kovaciny for his D.A. paper -- we appreciate his taking the time to seriously consider a subject which many today ignore, to their own hurt.

Charles D. Provan

CHAPTER THREE

PROTESTANT
THEOLOGIANS
AND
THE ONAN INCIDENT

Compiled and Edited by

Charles D. Provan

Today you find many people who do not want to have children. More-over, this callousness and inhuman attitude, which is worse than barbarous, is met with chiefly among the nobility and princes, who often refrain from marriage for this one single reason, that they might have no offspring. It is even more disgraceful that you find princes who allow themselves to be forced not to marry, for fear that the members of their house would increase beyond a definite limit. Surely such men deserve that their memory be blotted out from the land of the living. Who is there who would not detest these swinish monsters? But these facts, too, serve to emphasize original sin. Otherwise we would marvel at procreation as the greatest work of God, and as a most outstanding gift we would honor it with the praises it deserves.

Martin Luther

INTRODUCTION TO CHAPTER THREE

Many times we have heard discussions of Birth Control reduced to "Catholics" versus "Protestants". The "Defenders of Protestant Theology", as they style themselves, will state something along the lines that "Oh, well, Roman Catholic tradition is in opposition to contraception, but we Protestants follow the Bible, not tradition. That is why Protestants allow Birth Control." We have even seen books which state that Luther and Calvin laid the groundwork for Birth Control by de-emphasizing the connection between sexual intercourse and children. This assertion, which would not see the light of day were it not for the fact of gross ignorance of the Bible and Church history, is absolutely false. As we have seen in Chapter One, Calvin thought that Birth Control was murder, and Luther viewed it as sodomy.

Since we have heard the above view of "Bible Believers" vs. "Traditionalist Catholics" quite often, we thought that it would be profitable to research the Reformed view of contraception. The results which we encountered were, in our view, greatly heartening, for the views of the Reformers and their heirs were strongly opposed to Birth Control: we found that the historic Protestant opinion of Birth Control was to view it as unnatural, murderous and sodomitical, as well as a gross sin against God, the Church and Mankind.

We agree with the opponents of Dispensationalism, who often point to the fact that no one at all taught the pre-tribulation rapture view before about 1830, thus demonstrating its great weakness. We will go one better, and state that we have found not one orthodox theologian to defend Birth Control before the 1900's. NOT ONE! On the other hand, we have found that many highly regarded Protestant theologians were enthusiastically opposed to it, all the way back to the very beginning of the Reformation. We are pleased to associate ourselves with so respected a group of theologians. We are also pleased that those in favor of Birth Control will find no one in the orthodox Protestant camp for the first four centuries to ally themselves with.

We hope that present day Christians who advocate "family planning" will investigate the origins of the Birth Control movement, find it to be grossly immoral and anti-Christian, and return to the faith of their fathers. This is our earnest desire.

In our search for the Protestant view of Birth Control, we concentrated mainly upon Genesis 38, which is the story of Onan. We did this because of the fact that it is the only Bible passage to explicitly mention a specific form of contraception. Though we often moved into related sexual passages such as Gen. 1:28, 2:18, Psa. 127 and Romans 1, thereby discovering even more opponents of Birth Control, we have felt it best, due to space limitations, to list only those commentators who dealt with contraception via the Onan story. In this way, we may thus discover what was "the Protestant view of Onan". For the purposes of completeness, however, we have also included an appendix at the end, which lists the names of other Protestant theologians known to have opposed Birth Control. To paraphrase the Book of Hebrews, "since we are surrounded by so great a cloud of witnesses", may our opponents hearken unto our spiritual ancestors, and re-examine their own views. May our homes be blessed by true blessings which last. May our Holy Church be built up and strengthened. May God be honored by our conduct. Amen.

A POSTSCRIPT ON SELF-ABUSE

Though many today will affirm the non-sinfulness of masturbation, please notice the great frequency with which our spiritual forebears vehemently condemned it. Self-abuse, as many called it, is described as unnatural, perverse and vile, etc. Our readers may question why Onan's deed is used as a springboard for attacks on masturbation, sodomy, and other unclean practices. The reason is this: to our Christian ancestors, the sexual organs were designed by God to perform the sacred function of procreation: any voluntary use of the sexual organs which thwarted this goal was viewed as grossly wicked. Sodomy deposits semen outside the fruitful womb; does not masturbation do the same thing? In sodomy (as well as other forms of unnatural sexual relations) the principle of pleasure reigns supreme, with the negation of procreation; does not masturbation have the same characteristic? Thus, Onan was seen as a despicable character who was killed for wasting seed, a sin which applies to masturbators, sodomites, and those who practice Birth Control. Doubtless, this conclusion will certainly shock those who have imbibed heavily of modern-day "Christian" sex manuals. Nevertheless, this is where the Reformers and their followers stood on the subject.

As an aside, though a thousand surveys say that 99% of men masturbate, this does not prove the naturalness of masturbation. It is obvious that God has not created the sexual organs for masturbation, or else Paul would have said, "it is better to masturbate than to burn" instead of "it is better to marry than to burn". (1 Cor. 7:9)

Charles D. Provan

PROTESTANT THEOLOGIANS
ON THE ONAN INCIDENT

AINSWORTH, HENRY (1571-1622); Nonconformist
Commentary on Gen. 38:9 --
SPILLED] Or "corrupted", which the Greek translateth, "shed" (or spilled.) An unkind, and most unnatural fact; to spill the seed, which by God's blessing should serve for the propagation of mankind; and in this man, for the propagation of the Son of God according to the flesh, in whom all nations of the earth should be blessed, Gen. 22:18. which made the sin most impious, and hastened Onan's speedy death from the hand of God.

ALFORD, HENRY (1810-1871); Anglican
Commentary on Gen. 38 and 38:7 --
XXXVIII. The history of Judah and his daughter-in-law Tamar. The object of this parenthetical chapter seems to be to show how near the offspring of Jacob were to falling into the habits and loathsome sins of the Canaanitish peoples;
7] There is no detailed explanation of the reason of the death of Er, but it would seem by what follows, ver. 10, to have been something connected with the peculiar sins which brought destruction on the Canaanitish races.

ALTING, JACOB (1618-1679); Calvinist
Commentary on Gen. 38:7-10 --
Note Well: What kind of sin Er's was is uncertain. Some think it was the same as Onan's, but for a different reason; Er, lest Thamar should conceive and give birth and something of her beauty be lost; Onan, because she would have borne children not for himself but for his brother. The result of this union, the deed of Onan - because he was not seeking children for himself he did not want to procreate any lest he should procreate them for his brother. Verse 9. Onan's fate; the indignation of God for this deed and the just punishment of death inflicted, verse 10.

BARTH, CHRISTIAN GOTTLOB (1799-1862); Protestant
Commentary on Gen. 38 --
The narrative here advances from one sin to another. Judah, by his marriage with a Canaanitish woman, has sons of a dissolute character, whom God sees it necessary to remove prematurely from this life. Onan, who has given his name to a far-spread and widely-desolating crime, acted a doubly guilty part, inasmuch as he treated with contempt a holy ordinance and the promise of the kingdom of God. That promise of the seed of the woman, with which, after the death of the elder brother, he was closely concerned, was a matter of indifference to him. For this reason he also was cut off by the Lord.

BENGEL, JOHANN ALBRECHT (1687-1752); Lutheran
Commentary on Rom. 1:24, 26 --
AMONG THEIR OWN SELVES], by fornication, effeminacy [Bengel means "masturbators" here, as may be observed from his comments on 1 Cor. 6:9; C.P.], and other vices. They themselves furnish the materials of their own punishment, and are at the cost of it.
LUSTS OF DISHONOUR] [VILE AFFECTIONS -- English version] See Gerber's book: "Unknown Sins", Vol. 1, Chapter 92; "On Secret Vices". The writings of the heathen are full of such things. [Gerber's comments on Onan (to which Bengel here refers) are present in this list under "Gerber"; C.P.]

BROOKS, KEITH LEROY (1888- ?); Evangelical
Commentary on Gen. 38 --
Contents: Shame of Judah and his sons.
Conclusion: The sins which dishonor God and defile the body are evidences of vile affection and are very displeasing to God, often visited with quick punishment.

BROWN, JOHN (1722-1787); Presbyterian
Commentary on Gen. 38:9 --
His sin was extremely heinous, not only as it proceeded from envy of his brother's honor, and contempt of the promised seed, but as it was horrid and unnatural in itself. Nor to the last judgment will it appear what guilt of this nature hath been committed among mankind, nor how fearfully God hath punished the same.

BRUNNEMAN, JOHANNES (1608-1672); Lutheran
On Unnamed Vices --
There are some vices which one may not well name before chaste ears, but which still sneak around among the Christian people as we have often perceived from their judicial documents, academic opinions, and common talk, and sufficient reasons. So even the Onanitic sin and malicious spilling of seed occurs more than one probably imagines. It often occurs that unmarried fellows confess that they have known women carnally and yet deny that the woman is pregnant by them. If one asks how they might know that, so much finally comes out that one indeed hears that Onanitic vices have been committed (which is still more wicked than whoredom itself), and I remember that some have confessed in embarassing documents how they have practiced in lying together the evil artificial trick of Onan and have spilled it, from which and other abhorrent sins may God preserve the House of Jacob! Sirach 23. But I do not consider it adviseable in the pulpit to pass over these and other sins with total silence, but it is much rather necessary to present them thus

at times, though with modesty and caution, and to warn against them so that those who are aware of such sins in themselves or perhaps in others, as if nothing has led them astray to it, understand what the preacher means and how they should avoid such sin as one of the greatest. On July 30, 1668, a case in point of Sodomy was presented to us to pronounce judgment about it, in which he who had committed Sodomy was twenty-three years old and took a serious oath before God that he did not know that it was a sin to join with a sheep, goat, cow, or other beast, which ignorance, although it is very great, is to some extent alleged and protected in those handed down criminal documents. But from where else did this ignorance of this man come but precisely from this: that he had never heard such horrible sins rebuked from the pulpit?

BUSH, GEORGE (1796-1858); Presbyterian
Commentary on Gen. 38:9-10 --
9,10. IT CAME TO PASS WHEN HE WENT IN, &c. The motive of Onan's perverse conduct is clearly intimated in the first clause of the verse .... Such a conduct, moreover, in the present instance was peculiarly aggravated from the fact, that the Messiah was to descend from the stock of Judah, and for aught he knew, from himself, as we know he certainly did from this very Tamar, Mat. 1:3. Was it not then doing despite to the covenant-promise thus to crush in embryo the most sacred hopes of the world?

CALOVIUS, ABRAHAM (1612-1686); Lutheran
Commentary on Gen. 38:9-10 --
v. 9 BUT WHEN ONAN KNEW THAT THE SEED [the child] WOULD NOT BE HIS OWN, IF HE LAY WITH HIS BROTHER'S WIFE, HE LET IT FALL ON THE GROUND AND DESTROYED IT SO THAT HE WOULD NOT GIVE SEED TO HIS BROTHER.
v. 10 THAT WHICH HE DID DISPLEASED THE LORD AND HE KILLED HIM, TOO.
(That must have been a willful, desperate fellow, for this is always a shameful sin, yet much more atrocious than a case of incest or adultery: we call it a sin of the effeminate, indeed, even a sin of Sodomy. He was completely en-flamed with evil envy and jealousy, and that is why he would not permit himself to be forced to bear this simple service. Therefore it was quite right for God to kill him.)

CALVIN, JOHN (1509-1564); Calvinist
Commentary on Gen. 38:8-10 --
Besides, he [Onan; C.P.] not only defrauded his brother of the right due him, but also preferred his semen to putrify on the ground, rather than to beget a

son in his brother's name.

v. 10: The Jews quite immodestly gabble concerning this thing. It will suffice for me briefly to have touched upon this as much as modesty in speaking permits. The voluntary spilling of semen outside of intercourse between man and woman is a monstrous thing. Deliberately to withdraw from coitus in order that semen may fall on the ground is doubly monstrous. For this is to extinguish the hope of the race and to kill before he is born the hoped-for offspring. This impiety is especially condemned, now by the Spirit through Moses' mouth, that Onan, as it were, by a violent abortion, no less cruelly than filthily cast upon the ground the offspring of his brother, torn from the maternal womb. Besides, in this way he tried, as far as he was able, to wipe out a part of the human race. If any woman ejects a foetus from her womb by drugs, it is reckoned a crime incapable of expiation and deservedly Onan incurred upon himself the same kind of punishment, infecting the earth by his semen, in order that Tamar might not conceive a future human being as an inhabitant of the earth.

CANDLISH, ROBERT S. (1806-1873); Calvinist
Commentary on Gen. 38 --
The unnatural crime by means of which the wicked and wretched young man sought, and sought successfully, to defraud his deceased brother and defeat his father's ordinance - or rather the ordinance of his father's God, - while it stands out conspicuously, in the record of its swift and terrible doom, as a warning against all abuse of appetite, - is, at the same time, a proof of the depth and strength of his repugnance to what was required of him as an act of fraternal duty.

CLARKE, ADAM (1762?-1832); Methodist/Arminian
Commentary on Gen. 38:9-10 --
(9) The sin of self pollution, which is generally considered to be that of Onan, is one of the most destructive evils ever practised by fallen man. In many respects it is far worse than common whoredom, and has in its train more awful consequences; though practised by such as would shudder at the thought of criminal connection with a prostitute.... Worse woes than my pen can relate, I have witnessed in this engrossing, unnatural and most destructive of crimes.... God, and God alone, can save thee from an evil which has in its issue the destruction of thy body, and the final perdition of thy soul! Whether this may have been the sin of Onan, or not, is a matter at present of small moment; it may be thy sin: therefore take heed, lest God slay thee for it.

DANNHAUER, CONRAD (1603-1666); Lutheran

On Silent Unchastity, Effeminacy, Incest, Sodomy, and Foreign Marriage --

In general the silent unchastity is called "enallage geneseos", a change of the nature of the genital members and errors or the disorderly, irregular use of the same; and it includes the following vices: effeminacy, incest, sodomy, and foreign marriage. May the chaste Spirit grant us power and grace to treat this matter modestly and fittingly but to the extent necessary. Amen. Amen.

So now the first silent unchastity is [in Latin; C.P.] "mollities" and [in German; C.P.] "effeminacy" and "softness", the impurity par excellence, the abuse of the body in itself, as the Apostle calls it , which is otherwise also called the Onanistic sin. It is nothing other than an actual unchastity which the person arouses and commits with his member alone, without joining with another person.

I say "arouses" because what the nature and its drive does without the person's consent and whorish imaginings does not belong in this category, as also that does not belong here which happens unknowingly in sleep.

Unless the person habitually occupied himself with such unchaste thoughts and fantasies or also went to sleep with them or even full of them or did not well guard himself in bed against the enticements of the devil and the drive of original sin, which does not rest even in sleep; in which case such a person is one of those obscene dreamers, about whom St. Jude speaks, who soil the flesh, are companions of the Sodomites, and go after strange flesh. (1 Cor. 6:9; Eph. 5:3; Rom. 1:24...Jude 7, 8.)

Although these vices were in previous times not viewed or considered as great and horrible but were even allowed not only by the heathen philosophers (see Jerome on Eph. 5:3), especially by the doghead Diogenes the Cynic ["cynic" is Greek for "canine"; J.D.], who allowed all carnal arousal and semen flow; not only by the old wild brawlers called the Gnostics [on this see Ephiphanius haeres. 26.]; but also by the teachers in the Papacy (see Navarr. manual. c. 16. p. m, 232. Tolet. 1. 5. instruct. sacerd. c. 131.) Therefore also the same unchastity was much practiced in the cloisters and convents: some father confessors should confess what some brothers and sisters told them privately: indeed if one would, as Bernard [of Clairvaux; J.D.] speaks, according to the prophecy of Ezekiel, "bore through the walls and barriers of the cloisters and cells and take a look", what evil desire, wildness, and atrocity would one see? Although, I say, this sin is considered insignificant, indeed, a speck of dust, in the eyes of the world and of the whole of Babylon, it is still in the holy and chaste eyes of God an exceedingly abhorrent and shameful atrocity, more offensive than common whoredom and adultery; because it is more monstrous and runs contrary to nature and God's order. This sin is really an advance murder of that which could have been born of it. Indeed, such filthy persons thereby offer a Molech-sacrifice to the god of the whorish spirit, as the heathen in previous times sacrificed their seed to the idol Molech. May God, by His good Spirit, guard young hearts that they may be on guard against these snares of the devil so that they are not ensnared...and later fall totally into open shame and vice.

DEFOE, DANIEL (c.1657-1731); Nonconformist
On Matrimonial Chastity --
[Defoe quotes Jeremy Taylor on Onan.]

DODD, WILLIAM (1729-1777); Anglican
Commentary on Gen. 38:6-7 --
It is not said, who or of what family Tamar was, though it is most probable she was a Canaanitess: nor does it appear what was the crime of Er, enormous enough, no doubt, to draw down so exemplary a punishment from God. It is plain, from this transaction, that the practice, which Moses afterward enacted into law (Deut. 25:5) was of ancient standing; the same custom prevailed amongst the Egyptians. The crime of Onan shows a peculiarly malignant disposition (verse 9), and it is probable, that bad as it was in itself, yet his sin was aggravated with a worse circumstance, viz. his having an eye to the suppressing of the Messiah's birth, since he should not have the honor to be numbered among his ancestors, which might provoke God to cut him off. See Universal History. Acts of self pollution were always held particularly criminal, even by heathen moralists. The Hebrew doctors looked upon them as a degree of murder.

DORT, SYNOD OF (The Dutch Annotations upon the whole Bible...ordered and appointed by the Synod of Dort, 1618, and published by authority, 1637); Calvinist
Commentary on Gen. 38:9 --
9. YET ONAN, KNOWING [See the notes on the precedent verse] THAT THIS SEED, [i.e. Son; see above Chap. 4. on ver. 25.] SHOULD NOT BE FOR HIM, IT HAPPENED, WHEN HE WENT IN TO HIS BROTHER'S WIFE, THAT HE SPILLED IT AGAINST THE GROUND, [or, defiled it, etc. The Hebrew word signifying both the one and the other: this was even as much, as if he had (in a manner) pulled forth the fruit out of the mother's womb, and destroyed it.] NOT TO GIVE SEED TO HIS BROTHER.

EDERSHEIM, ALFRED (1825-1889); Presbyterian
Commentary on Genesis 38 --
How readily constant contact with the Canaanites would have involved even the best of them in horrible vices appears from the history of Judah, when after the selling of Joseph, he had left his father's house, and, joining himself to the people of the country, both he and his rapidly became conformed to the abominations around.

ELTON, EDWARD (1637)
Commentary on Col. 3:5 --
Now the second sin here named is uncleanness. This sin also is an outward breach of the Seventh Commandment. And by it we are to understand every actual defilement of body against nature. As that of incest with such as are within degrees forbidden and laid forth in Lev. 18:6-18. And of other defilements which are more against nature: as that which is committed with another kind (as with brute beasts), expressly forbidden in Lev. 18:23; or that which is committed with that sex which is not for that natural use spoken of in Rom. 1:26-27 and which was the sin of sodomy; or that which is most unnatural and was in part the sin of Onan (Gen. 38:9). Now these defilements of the body are most foul and grievous sins in that they are not only against the law of God and against the very light of nature -- they are commonly punishments of some other horrible sins and ever follow a very profane and dead heart. (Rom. 1:24).

EXELL, JOSEPH S. (1849-c.1909); Reformed
Commentary on Gen 38:8-10 --
Vers. 8-10. Onan -- The sin of Onan:
III. It was a dishonour done to his own body. [Here Exell quotes the entire comments of Leale and Hughes; C.P.]

FRITZ, JOHN H.C. (1874-1953); Lutheran
On Marriage --
Relation of Parents and Children - Two things a pastor should impress upon married people: 1. that God would bless their marriage with children; 2. that God holds parents responsible for the Christian training of their children. A husband and a wife should according to God's will become the father and the mother of children. One of God's purposes of marriage is the propagation of the human race. God says: "Be fruitful and multiply and replenish the earth," Gen. 1:28; Ps. 127 and 128; Fourth Commandment. A Hebrew married woman considered it an affliction to be childless, 1 Sam. 1:1-20. The Jews had large families; so did our German forefathers. The one-, two-, or three-children family system is contrary to the Scriptures; for man has no right arbitrarily or definitely to limit the number of his offspring (birth control), especially not if done with artificial or unnatural means, Gen. 1:28; Ps. 127:3-6; Ps. 128:3-4; Gen. 38:9-10. Such restrictions as uncontrollable circumstances, natural barrenness, or the ill health of wife or husband put upon the number of offspring are the exceptions to the rule. Child-bearing is both a natural and a healthful process, while any interference with natural functions is injurious.

GERBER, CHRISTIAN (1660-1731); Lutheran
On Secret Unchastity

Sec. 3. But among the types of secret unchastity one must properly include the impurity with which mean spirits dirty their bodies and wound their consciences even when they are alone and do not even carnally join with someone else. St. Paul calls such people effeminate (1 Cor. 6:9), who may lay hands on themselves and commit with their genitals such abhorrent things that one does not want to think about it, much less speak about it. And to the best of my memory, I have heard such stories about it that not only males do such things and maliciously, indeed, abhorrently "spill the seed", as Scripture speaks [Gen. 38:8-10; C.P.]; but that even the feminine gender lets itself be led astray by the impure, infernal spirit to think of means whereby they can satisfy their impure desires and themselves still the raging passion. Forgive me, my reader, for writing this. I do so most unwillingly. But I am forced by the great need and the danger of so many souls. Oh! it is with this horrible thing that the heathen have made themselves impure and perhaps do so still. I have read of certain heathen philosophers that they have studiously withheld themselves from the use of women but on the contrary have committed with their hands impurity such as not even any beast does. Jac. a Reis in Campo Jucundar. Qu. p.m. 569, qu. 46. n. 15. writes about Diogenes the Cynic in this way; -- whence it must be gathered that Diogenes' depravity and illegitimacy reached such an extent that he frequently used his hand as a substitute for the feminine hymen for the sake of satiety: -- wherefore even the guilty Galenus, who had been most continent, then no longer wanted to serve this continence and became more of an infamous masturbator. But perhaps Galenus was just such a fellow as Diogenes and thought that one was already chaste and decent if one only did not join with a woman even though otherwise an improper thing is done with the private member.

Sec. 4. These heathen atrocities are truthfully not rare among us now. One would not believe what some youths and even men do under cover and what kinds of shameful acts they pursue. It was about two or three years ago that the conscience of an unmarried man awoke and forced him to confess to two close friends that he had committed unchastity and impurity against himself, about which his soul was enduring an indescribable anxiety. Indeed, this man confessed that he had learned this wickedness at a famous school in a major city, which he had attended in his youth , where most of the pupils practiced this same devilish impurity with themselves. Oh, it may be complained to God that Satan has made also such nurseries so horribly impure! Oh, that we had enough water and that our eyes were wells of tears in order sufficiently to lament such inhuman unchastity and atrocity. Those are the sins with which the heathen have made themselves impure: "For this cause God gave them up unto vile affections: for even their women did change the natural use into that which is against nature: And likewise also the men, leaving the natural use of the woman, burned in their lust one toward another; men with men working that which is unseemly, and receiving in themselves that recompence of their error which was meet." Rom. 1:26-27. Because of these sins, God destroyed the inhabitants of Sodom with fire from heaven, and they are still burning to this hour in hellfire. Because of these sins, God also destroyed the Canaanites and put the children of Israel into the land in their place. So if one will only pay attention to it, the well known saying always applies: "The vices of the seed are punished in the seed." In Leviticus 15, God commanded: If the seed goes out of a man in his sleep, he should wash his whole flesh with water and be unclean until the evening. So if the holy God is displeased by the spilling of the seed which occurs outside of the legitimate cohabitation with the wife, as Osiander glosses this passage: how much more before His holy eyes will it be an atrocity when such is done maliciously and intentionally. In summary: the atrocity is so great that it cannot be expressed.

Sec. 5. But therefore, O youths and men, for the sake of the unique Son of Mary and His five holy wounds, let yourselves be implored to guard yourselves against making your bodies impure, as dear to you as your salvation is. Oh, but consider that nothing impure shall enter the kingdom of God. Then where would you want to remain? Although you are alone and no one sees or knows anything of your shameful acts, God still sees, Whose eyes are brighter than the sun. The angels see it and depart from such impure spirits as you are. The devil sees it, and at the end of your life he will cite you, so to speak, before God and accuse you because of your shaming of your own bodies. Your conscience sees it and will in its time miserably torture you for it. Or have you then completely forgotten that in Baptism you renounced the devil and all his impure works and have put on Christ? Do you not know that your body is to be the temple of the Holy Spirit? Oh, how many devils may be around you when you secretly commit such impurity? Once I saw certain citizens together in one place drinking. They told one another such things with laughing mouths, what they sometimes undertook with their wives and how they had also done otherwise, so that I now cannot otherwise judge than that the devil himself at that time sat in their hearts and on their tongues. O you impure heathen, why do you let yourselves be called Christians? With what kind of conscience can you go to the holy Supper? And do you not shy away from receiving the most holy body and blood of Christ with your impure lips? Oh, woe to you to all eternity! Preachers do not like to talk about it from the pulpit and therefore seldom do so. But to that extent these abhorrent sins take the upper hand so that preachers truly need to rebuke the same more often with great earnestness and movingly to warn against them.

Now what these old theologians have done stands free also for me and other faithful preachers to do, especially since many are not so pure from Sodomitic atrocities. When in the year 1687 I came to speak with the deacon there in Toeplitz in Bohemia, I met with the same rebuke: did we not instruct our people all too little so that the common man often did not know what was sin?

Now since the adversaries rebuke us for such things, then I ask whether it is not necessary to warn the people against Onanitic and other mute sins, especially since the Holy Spirit Himself does not pass over such sins in silence but has them shown in the case of godless Onan, Gen. 38:9. What else certain Christian wives have complained to me about, how their husbands were accustomed to act with them, I should not report here because of modesty.

GERHARD, JOHANN (1582-1637); Lutheran
Commentary on Gen. 38:7-10 --
Most Hebrew and Christian interpreters conclude that the sin of Er was of the same type as the sin of Onan, which they call effeminacy. Augustine in book 22, Against Faust Chap. 84, concluded that this Er had sinned in this offense severely, because that sin impedes conception and destroys the foetus in its own seed.

God detests and punishes shameful acts. Shortness-of-life for the wicked is the punishment of sins. The sin of effeminacy and voluntary pouring out of seed is contrary to nature: this in itself is compared by the Hebrews to homicide. Thomas argues that this is more serious than homicide.

[Augustine (354-430) had this to say about Onan's sin: "And why has Paul said: 'If he cannot control himself, let him marry'? Surely, to prevent incontinence from constraining him to adultery. If, then, he practices continence, neither let him marry nor beget children. However, if he does not control himself, let him enter into lawful wedlock, so that he may not beget children in disgrace or avoid having offspring by a more degraded form of intercourse. There are some lawfully wedded couples who resort to this last, for intercourse, even with one's lawfully wedded spouse, can take place in an unlawful and shameful manner, whenever the conception of offspring is avoided. Onan, the son of Juda, did this very thing, and the Lord slew him on that account. Therefore, the procreation of children is itself the primary, natural, legitimate purpose of marriage. Whence it follows that those who marry because of their inability to remain continent ought not to so temper their vice that they preclude the good of marriage, which is the procreation of children.";
C.P.]

GILL, JOHN (1697-1771); Nonconformist
Commentary on Gen. 38:9-10
AND ONAN KNEW THAT THE SEED SHOULD NOT BE HIS;--Should not be called a son of his, but a son of his brother Er; this is to be understood only of the first-born; all the rest of the children born afterwards were reckoned the children of the real parent of them; this shews this was a custom in use in those times, and well known; and was not a peculiar case; AND IT CAME TO PASS, WHEN HE WENT IN UNTO HIS BROTHER'S WIFE; to cohabit with her, as man and wife, he having married her according to his father's direction: THAT HE SPILLED it ON THE GROUND, LEST HE SHOULD GIVE HIS SEED TO HIS BROTHER; lest his brother's wife he had married should conceive by him, and bear a son that should be called his brother's and inherit his estate; and this is the sin which from him is called Onania, a sin condemned by the light of nature, as well as by the word of God, and very prejudicial to mankind, as well as displeasing to God, as follows: AND THE THING WHICH HE DID DISPLEASED THE LORD: - Being done out of envy to his brother, and through want of affection to the memory of his name; and it may be out of covetousness, to get his estate into his own hands, and especially as it frustrated the end of such an usage of marrying a brother's wife; which appears to be according to the will of God, since it afterwards became a known law of his; and it was the more displeasing, as it was not only a check upon the multiplication of Abraham's seed, as promised, but since the Messiah was to come from Judah. This was doing all to hinder it that lay in his power: wherefore HE SLEW HIM ALSO; in like manner as he had slain his brother.

HALL, JOSEPH (1574-1656); Anglican
Commentary on Gen. 38 --
His brother Onan sees the judgment, and yet follows his sins. Every little thing discourages us from good; nothing can alter the heart that is set upon evil. Er was not worthy of any love; but though he were a miscreant, yet he was a brother. Seed should have been raised to him; Onan justly loses his life with his seed, which he would rather spill, than lend to a wicked brother. ...What difference God puts betwixt sins of wilfulness and infirmity! The son's pollution is punished with present death; the father's incest is pardoned, and in a sort prospereth.

HENRY, MATTHEW (1662-1714); Nonconformist
Commentary on Gen. 38:1-11 --
Onan, though he consented to marry the widow, yet to the great abuse of his own body, of the wife that he had married, and of the memory of his brother that was gone, he refused to raise up seed unto his brother, as he was in duty

bound. This was so much the worse because the Messiah was to descend from Judah, and had he not been guilty of this wickedness, he might have had the honour of being one of his ancestors. Note, Those sins that dishonour the body and defile it are very displeasing to God and evidences of vile affections.

HUGHES, GEORGE (1603-1667); Nonconformist
Commentary on Gen. 38:8-10 --
The fact itself, AND IT WAS, HE WENT IN UNTO HIS BROTHER'S WIFE, THAT HE SPILLED IT ON THE EARTH.... Herein note many evils: 1. Uncleanness. 2. Self-pollution. 3. Destruction of future seed, which God ordered to be produced.

Lessons: --Vain parents take little knowledge of God's judgments in the death of one child when they have others. 2. Special law for the marriage of the deceased brother's wife by the brother was given of God for special ends. 3. Seed was much desirable and is so in the Church of God; for which such laws were made (ver. 8). 4. Wicked creatures are selfish in duty, therefore unwilling to seek any good but their own. 5. Self-pollution, destruction of the seed of man, envy to brethren, are Onan's horrid crimes (ver. 9). 6. Onans may be in the visible Church. 7. Such uncleanness is very grievous in God's sight. 8. Exemplary death may be expected from God by such transgressors (ver.10).

JACOBUS, MELANCTHON W. (1816-1876); Presbyterian
Commentary on Gen. 38:6-7 --
6-7. This wife of Er was probably a Canaanite also, and he was smitten to death by God for his wickedness. Whereupon his brother Onan was commanded by his father to act the part of husband to the widow according to the custom of Levirate marriage, afterwards legalized by Moses. In order that the family might not die out and the covenant line perish, this was an important provision. (Ruth 4:10) Onan, however, proved false, and his crime of violating God's ordinance by a shameful abomination was also punished with death. Thus the covenant household seems degraded and disgraced. But the salvation lies not with them but with God.

JENKYN, WILLIAM (1612-1685); Nonconformist
Commentary on Jude 7 --
"fornication;"....To mention therefore only the principal sorts of carnal uncleanness, and such as we find (though with sacred modesty) set down in Scripture. This sin, if practised with a man's own body, according to the opinion of some, is called "malakia", and "akatharsia", effeminateness and uncleanness, for which God slew Onan, Gen. 38:9; 1 Cor. 6:9; Col. 3:5;

Nor is it impossible but that uncleanness may be between married couples, when the use of the marriage bed is in a season prohibited, or in a measure not moderated, or in a manner not ordained, or to an end not warranted.

JUNIUS, FRANCISCUS (1545-1602); Calvinist editor of the Belgic Confession; theological opponent of Jacob Arminius.
Commentary on Gen. 38:9 --
[9] The most ugly impudence, which is not even easily named among the heathen, but was once practiced by the Gnostics according to the testimony of Epiphanius.

[Two passages of Epiphanius of Salamis (c. 315-402) on the Gnostic heretics are as follows: "But though they copulate they forbid procreation. Their eager pursuit of seduction is for enjoyment, not procreation, since the devil mocks people like these, and makes fun of the creature fashioned by God." "...the Gnostics' wickedness. Whether they perform their filthy act with men or women, they still forbid insemination, thus doing away with the procreation God has given his creatures - as the apostle says, 'receiving in themselves the recompense of their error which was meet', and so on. (Rom. 1:27)" For a passage by Epiphanius which mentions the Gnostics and Onan together, see our listing of Richard Stock.; C.P.]

KEIL AND DELITSZCH
KEIL, JOHANN KARL FRIEDRICH (1807-1888); Lutheran
DELITSZCH, FRANZ (1813-1890); Lutheran
Commentary on Gen. 38:8-10 --
Judah then wished Onan, as the brother-in-law, to marry the childless widow of his deceased brother, and raise up seed, i.e. a family, for him. But as he knew that the first-born son would not be the founder of his own family, but would perpetuate the family of the deceased and receive his inheritance, he prevented conception when consummating the marriage by spilling the semen. ..."DESTROYED TO THE GROUND (i.e. let it fall upon the ground), SO AS NOT TO GIVE SEED TO HIS BROTHER".... This act not only betrayed a want of affection to his brother, combined with a despicable covetousness for his possession and inheritance, but was also a sin against the divine institution of marriage and its object, and was therefore punished by Jehovah with sudden death.

KIDDER, RICHARD (? -1703); Anglican
Commentary on Gen. 38 --
Should not be called his or should not be called by his name as the Chaldee renders it well. Thus envy carries him to another great sin.

KRETZMANN, PAUL E. (1883-1965); Lutheran
Commentary on Gen. 38:9 --

V. 9 AND ONAN KNEW THAT THE SEED SHOULD NOT BE HIS, that a possible first-born son would not perpetuate his name and family, but that of his brother Er; AND IT CAME TO PASS, WHEN HE WENT IN UNTO HIS BROTHER'S WIFE, THAT HE SPILLED IT ON THE GROUND, LEST THAT HE SHOULD GIVE SEED TO HIS BROTHER. Rather than yield to the custom and be obedient to his father, Onan committed this crime against the divine institution of marriage and its purpose according to the will of God. Such works of the flesh, all too prevalent in our day, when children are no longer desired, are an abomination before the Lord. Where the fear of God still rules, such vices will not be tolerated.

LAETSCH, THEODORE F. K. (1877-1962); Lutheran
ARGUMENTS AGAINST BIRTH CONTROL
1. It is sinful.
A. It is wilfully setting aside God's will and command, Gen. 1:28; 1 Tim. 5:14; 2:15; Gen. 38:9-10.
B. It is despising His promises and is depriving oneself of a blessing, Ps. 127 and 128. See texts under C.
C. It is usurping for oneself an exclusive privilege of God, that of giving or withholding children, Ps. 127:3; Gen. 29:31-30:6; 30:22; 33:5; 16:2; 20:18; Lev. 20:20-21; Job 42:12-13; Luke 1:58; 1 Sam. 1:10-11.
D. Birth Control by means of anticonceptuals, coitus interruptus, etc. is ruthlessly interfering with God's method of creating a living being. Hufeland, one of the most noted physicians of Germany, 1762-1836, says: "The first question undoubtedly is, When does life begin? There can be no doubt that the act of copulation is to be regarded as the beginning of the existence of the future being and that the very first, even though invisible, germ of this being has the same claim upon the care and protection of the physician as the later, fully developed man... A human being is being murdered in its incipiency. I am not going to answer sophistic, even Jesuitic, cavils. I appeal to sane reason and to the pure, unspoiled moral feeling of every man...The product presupposes producing, and if it is wrong to kill the product, then it goes without saying that it is wrong to render futile the act whereby it is being produced, for thereby one actually kills that which is in process of being produced (das Werdende) in its first beginning." Quoted in De Valenti, Die Ehe, biblisch und aerztlich beleuchtet, page 65 f. This is undoubtedly the Scriptural view. Cf. Ps. 139:13-16; Job 10:8-11, especially v. 10 (the act of copulation described).
E. Marriage degenerates from a holy estate to mere gratification of carnal lust, Heb. 13:4; 1 Thess. 4:4.
2. It undermines the State. It is race suicide. Even the two-children system will rapidly lead to extermination of a people, for 10 per cent. of all marriages are

naturally childless, and unmarried people do not contribute to the growth of a nation, while the two-children system replaces only the parents, no replacements for unmarried people and childless couples, hence a decrease in population, and the nation will die out. At least four children to a family to prevent this dying out, five children to bring about an increase in population. 3. It undermines the home. Parents become selfish, incompatible. Children idolized, pampered, egotistic, self-important, undesirable citizens in many instances. A Supreme Court Justice is quoted as saying: "It is my conclusion that childless homes are responsible for the almost complete absence of real home-life. I cannot help but reach the conclusion that, if our women had children, there would be more happiness and fewer divorces. Presence of children attracts the husband to his home and keeps the mothers from the gossiping neighbors and bridge parties. Absence of children promotes discord. Their presence makes for harmony."

LANGE, JOHANN PETER (1802-1884); Reformed
Commentary on Gen. 38:8-10 --
Onan's sin, a deadly wickedness, an example to be held in abhorrence, as condemnatory, not only of secret sins of self-pollution, but also of all similar offences in sexual relations, and even in marriage itself. Unchasitity in general is a homicidal waste of the generative powers, a demonic bestiality, an outrage to ancestors, to posterity, and to one's own life. It is a crime against the image of God, and a degradation below the animal. Onan's offence, moreover, as committed in marriage, was a most unnatural wickedness, and a grievous wrong. The sin named after him is destructive as a pestilence that walketh in darkness, destroying directly the body and soul of the young. But common fornication is likewise an unnatural violation of the person, a murder of two souls and a desecration of the body as the temple of God. There are those in our Christian communities who are exceedingly gross in this respect; a proof of the most defective development of what may be called, the consciousness of personality and of personal dignity.
[Here Lange quotes Schroder, who is in our listing, followed by the next quotation; C.P.]
Schwenke-The sin of Onan, unnatural, destructive of God's holy ordinance, is even yet so displeasing to the Lord that it gives birth to bodily and spiritual death.

LEALE, THOMAS H. (c. 1877); Evangelical
Commentary on Gen. 38:8-10 --
THE SIN OF ONAN - Verses 8-10
I. It was prompted by a low motive. It was as selfish as it was vile. Onan's design was to preserve the whole inheritance for his own house.

II. It was a act of willful disobedience to God's ordinance. "Ill deservings of others can be no excuse for our injustice, for our uncharitableness. That which Tamar required, Moses afterward, as from God, commanded -- the succession of brothers into the barren bed. Some laws God spake to His Church long ere He wrote them: while the author is certainly known, the voice and the finger of God are worthy of equal respect." --(Bp. Hall.)

III. It was a dishonour done to his own body. [This comment is followed by a quotation from Lange, who appears in our list; C.P.]

IV. It was aggravated by his position in the covenant family. The Messiah was to descend from the stock of Judah, and for aught he knew from himself. This very Tamar is counted in the genealogy of Christ. (Matt. 1:3) Herein he did despite to the covenant promise. He rejected an honourable destiny.

LEUPOLD, HERBERT CARL (1892-1972); Lutheran
Commentary on Gen. 38:8-10 --
The custom of levirate marriage seems to have prevailed quite universally at the time, as it is known to have been customary among many nations ancient and modern. Judah does not appear as an innovator in this instance. Levirate marriage implied that if a man had died without leaving a son, the next brother of the deceased, if unmarried, would take the widow to wife with the understanding that the first son born would carry on the line of the deceased, but all other children would be accounted his own. The Mosaic code refers to the custom Deut. 25:5 ff. and made what had previously been a custom among such as the Israelites a divine ordinance. See a further reference in Matt. 22:24. The root yabam means "brother-in-law." The Piel of the derivative verb could then be translated "marry her as brother-in-law", the ultimate purpose of course being "to raise up offspring" (Hebrew: "seed") to the brother. Onan knew of this provision and intentionally prevented its realization. Selfishness may have prompted him; he did not care to preserve his brother's family. Greed may have been a concurrent motive; he desired to prevent the division of the patrimony into smaller units. But in addition to these two faults there was palpably involved the sin of a complete perversion of the purpose of marriage, that divine institution. What he did is described as "taking preventative measures." The original says: "he destroyed (i.e. the semen) to the ground." From him the extreme sexual perversion called onanism has its name. The case is revolting enough. But plain speech in this case serves as a healthy warning.

LUTHER, MARTIN (1483-1546); Lutheran
Commentary on Gen. 38:8-10 --
...the exceedingly foul deed of Onan, the basest of wretches, follows.
9. BUT ONAN KNEW THAT THE OFFSPRING WOULD NOT BE HIS; SO WHEN HE WENT IN TO HIS BROTHER'S WIFE, HE SPILLED THE SEMEN

ON THE GROUND, LEST HE SHOULD GIVE OFFSPRING TO HIS BROTHER. 10. AND WHAT HE DID WAS DISPLEASING IN THE SIGHT OF THE LORD, AND HE SLEW HIM ALSO.

Onan must have been a malicious and incorrigible scoundrel. This is a most disgraceful sin. It is far more atrocious than incest and adultery. We call it unchastity, yes, a Sodomitic sin. For Onan goes in to her; that is, he lies with her and copulates, and when it comes to the point of insemination, spills the semen, lest the woman conceive. Surely at such a time the order of nature established by God in procreation should be followed. Accordingly, it was a most disgraceful crime to produce semen and excite the woman, and to frustrate her at that very moment. He was inflamed with the basest spite and hatred. Therefore he did not allow himself to be compelled to bear that intolerable slavery. Consequently, he deserved to be killed by God. He committed an evil deed. Therefore God punished him. ...That worthless fellow refused to exercise [love; C.P.]. He preferred polluting himself with a most disgraceful sin to raising up offspring for his brother.

Therefore Onan, unwilling to perform this obligation, spilled his seed. That was a sin far greater than adultery or incest, and it provoked God to such fierce wrath that He destroyed him immediately.

MAIER, WALTER ARTHUR (1893-1950); Lutheran
The Blight of Birth Control; Its Anti-Scriptural Bias

To pass over other objections to birth control, - objections so weighty that these sections of the Federal Penal Code make it a criminal offense, punishable by five years in jail or a fine of $5,000 or both, to send through the mails or through other common carriers "any article, drug or medicine, or any obscene, lewd or lascivious publication intended for preventing conception," - we come to the basic objection, which, if all other argumentation were swept aside, would be a complete denunciation. We refer to the evident indictment of birth control contained in the statements of Scripture.

The majority report of the Committee on Birth Control appointed by the Federal Council of the Churches of Christ in America states that the Church and the Bible are "silent upon the subject." This is a bold statement. When the first human parent pair was created, the divine command enjoined: "Be fruitful and multiply and replenish the earth." (Gen. 1:28). After the Deluge, when the world was to take its second start, the blessing for Noah and his sons again required them to "be fruitful and multiply and replenish the earth" (Gen. 9:1) In Ps. 127:3 we read: "Lo, children are an heritage of the Lord, And the fruit of the womb is His reward." The picture of the ideal home is described in Ps. 128:3: "Thy wife shall be as a fruitful vine by the sides of thine house, Thy children like olive plants round about thy table."

In Proverbs 31:28 children are mentioned as part of the virtuous woman's household. If it is objected that these are Old Testament passages, attention is called to these utterances of the New Testament: 1 Tim. 5:10, where it is stated that those aged widows who "brought up children" received support from the church; 1 Tim. 5:14, where the apostle directs the younger women (the widows) "to marry, bear children"; 1 Cor. 7:14, which illustrates God's gracious interest in His children's children; and particularly Mark 10:14, where the Savior of the race utters His memorable "Suffer the little children to come unto Me." In spite of extended argument not a single passage can be adduced from Scripture which even in any remote way condones birth control; and no one acquainted with the Bible should hesitate to admit that it is a definite departure from the requirements of Scripture. See Gen 38:9,10.

MATHER, COTTON (1663-1728); Calvinist
The Pure Nazarite --
It is time for me to tell you, that the Crime against which I warn you, is that Self-Pollution, which from the Name of the only Person that stands for ever stigmatiz'd for it in our Holy Bible, bears the Name of ONANISM.

MAYER, JOHN (1583-1664); Anglican
Commentary on Gen. 38:8-10
For the sin of Onan, it was most detestable. 1. Because it was unnatural to spill the seed given him for generation. 2. Because he did great wrong thus unto Tamar, hindering her, that she could not be the mother of children. 3. He did, as much as in him, mar the seminary of the generation of man, that he should have no further increased. 4. He was envious in the highest degree against his dead brother, rather than he would raise up seed unto him, he preferred to go himself seedless. Lastly it was also aggravated, in that Er being made an example for his wickedness before him, he would not yet take warning thereby, wherefore he was most justly by some remarkable judgement soon taken away also.

MERCIER, JEAN (c. 1500-1562); Huguenot, teacher of Ursinus
Commentary on Gen. 38 --
But since Onan realized that the seed would not be his own, or the descendants which he would beget from her, it came to pass, that is to say when he went in to his brother's wife to pollute (so to speak) himself or the seed poured out onto the ground, which means not to provide seed, that is, in order not to raise up progeny for his brother. In what manner that came to pass it seems difficult to comprehend and to express because it is obscene, but it is easily imagined: for in that union when it came to the point of the ejaculation of the seed, that seed was not ejaculated into its proper place, that is, the wife's womb, but it poured forth onto the earth, the result being that both she herself

and the deceased brother were defrauded of progeny. The sin was utterly contrary to nature and all respectibility, and it was foreign to the goal of marriage; therefore, it was justly punished by God: whence the Jews say that the man who pours out seed rashly is equal to the one who is guilty of homicide.

MURPHY, JAMES G. (1808-1896); Reformed
Commentary on Gen. 38:7,8 --
WAS EVIL IN THE EYES OF THE LORD. The God of covenant is obliged to cut off Er for his wickedness in the prime of life. We are not made acquainted with his crime; but it could scarcely be more vile and unnatural than that for which his brother Onan is also visited with death. AND BE A HUSBAND TO HER. The original word means to act as a husband to the widow of a deceased brother who has left no issue. Onan seems to have been prompted to commit his crime by the low motive of turning the whole inheritance to his own house.

MUSCULUS, WOLFGANG (1497-c.1563); Lutheran
Commentary on Gen. 38:9-10 --
It says three things: the deed of Onan, the reason for the deed, and the divine punishment. The deed was like this: "AND IT HAPPENED THAT WHEN HE WENT INTO HIS BROTHER'S WIFE, HE SPOILED IT ON THE GROUND"; his seed, that is, from which Thamar was supposed to conceive, he poured not into her womb but with outstanding malice onto the ground. The reason for the deed is stated in what is said, "ONAN, KNOWING THAT IT WOULD NOT BE HIS OWN OFFSPRING". Therefore, he disdained to help his brother, and for that reason he denied him his own seed. In this we see the nature of unbelieving man. What was about to come to his brother, he did not refuse so as to help himself, but instead he preferred to uselessly waste it, rather than give it to his brother. "Neither for my brother", he says "nor for a buzzard". [unsure "milu"? = Miluus, kite?; P.L.] But anyway he was able to help also himself if first he helped his brother. For the first born has certain claims regarding a brother which others do not. The divine punishment is thus reported: "AND WHAT HE DID WAS DISPLEASING IN THE EYES OF THE LORD, AND SO HE KILLED HIM". So the deed of Onan was cause for death. For he was sinning first against God himself, whose primary commandment he violated. Also he sinned against human nature, spilling seed from which she could have conceived and borne children. Third, against Israel and the people of God from which he detracted; and whose reproduction promised by God he ought to have multiplied. Fourth, against his father whose will and right he had defied. For he had been going into his own brother's wife and relieving his lust: but real offspring he held back from raising up for his brother, which is the one thing his father was asking. Fifth, he sinned against

his brother also, whose name and posterity in Israel, although he was able, he refused to save. Therefore, it is not beyond reason that what he did was so thoroughly condemned, even to the point that it was displeasing in the eyes of God so that he killed him.

Let all those be absolutely terrified by this example who thus relieve their lust, so that by no means, neither for themselves nor for others, especially not for anyone other than themselves, do they desire to bring forth offspring. Those who practice forbidden lust are most like the evildoer Onan. For they want nothing less than children. This type of person couples in various and un-speakable ways so as not to get the woman pregnant: and if she should get pregnant, somehow the foetus in her either in the womb or at birth is killed. Woe, woe on these lewd women -- woe, I say, on the prostitutes of the Sodomites, among whom no one is expected to be procreated, and what they do most wickedly is displeasing in the eyes of the Lord.

OLDENBURGER, TEUNIS (1934); Calvinist
Birth Control for Saints and Sinners

There is no other exegesis of Scripture possible but to place contraception in the same category with prostitution, free love, homosexuality, coitus interup-tus, coitus reservatus, coitus Saxonus, and all other forms of unnatural coition that are indulged in simply for the purpose of play, against which both the laws of the land and those of the Church have with varying severity been enforced, beginning with Onan in Chapter 38 of Genesis and extending to our own day among all civilized countries.

Birth Control is cursed of God as a sex crime, and, in the one case of which we have record, in Gen. 38 was punished with death.

OLEARIUS, JOHANNES (1611-1684); Lutheran
Commentary on Gen. 38:9 --

9. BUT SINCE ONAN KNEW THAT THE SEED WOULD NOT BE HIS OWN IF HE LAY WITH HIS BROTHER'S WIFE, HE LET IT FALL TO THE GROUND AND PERISH SO THAT HE WOULD NOT GIVE SEED TO HIS BROTHER.... This cursed, abhorrent sin, which was an atrocity against na-ture and against the Lord (as against the Most High, Is. 6, Who cannot tolerate even unintentional impurity, Lev. 15:16), happened secretly and was punished publicly. What Cain did to his brother, Gen. 4, that this murderous abuser of nature did, as much as he could, and it was no better. Therefore it displeased the Lord...just as David's adultery and murder, 2 Sam. 11:27. This wickedness deserves the wages of sin, Rom. 6, and early death... The atroc-ity of Molech, Lev. 20:2, is to be considered in this context. This matter, together with all silent sins, is not improperly compared to that situation.

OSIANDER, LUKAS, THE ELDER (1534-1604); Lutheran
Commentary on Gen. 38:10 --
WHAT HE DID] Which was an abhorrent thing and worse than adultery. For such an evil deed strives against nature, and those who do it will not possess the Kingdom of God, 1 Cor. 6:9-10. And the holier marriage is, the less will those remain unpunished who live in it in a wicked and unfitting way so that, in addition to it, they practice their private acts of villainy.

PARAEUS, DAVID (1548-1586); Calvinist
Commentary on Gen. 38 --
9. NEVERTHELESS ONAN KNEW
Detestable was the deed of Onan, who in sexual intercourse preferred to waste his seed rather than procreate children, lest he raise up offspring for his brother. For he knew that by custom the firstborn would not be his but his dead brother's. This was not only wicked jealousy for his brother but also savage cruelty, which God considered on the same level as parricide. For what is it to waste the seed other than kill the foetus and the human being that is to be born from it? Because of this he was justly killed by God, by a sudden blow, it seems, or by a fatal disease.
On the other hand we learn how much God hates every abuse of genital seed, illicit emission and wasting it: and we learn that we are to live chaste and holy lives before God in marriage just as much as in the celibate life. For God sees and punishes every impurity, even those which are committed in secret.

PATRICK, SIMON (1626-1707); Anglican
Commentary on Gen. 38:10 --
Ver. 10 THE THING WHICH HE DID DISPLEASED THE LORD:] This made his sin the more heinous, that he acted against the Divine promise made to Abram, concerning the multiplying of his seed: especially against the belief of the promise of the Messiah; that seed for which all good men longed.

POOLE, MATTHEW (1624-1679); Nonconformist
Commentary on Gen. 38:9 --
9. AND ONAN KNEW THAT THE SEED SHOULD NOT BE HIS; AND IT CAME TO PASS, WHEN HE WENT IN UNTO HIS BROTHER'S WIFE, THAT HE SPILLED IT ON THE GROUND, LEST THAT HE SHOULD GIVE SEED TO HIS BROTHER. Two things are here noted: 1. The sin itself, which is here particularly described by the Holy Ghost, that men might be instructed concerning the nature and the great evil of this sin of self-pollution, which is such that it brought upon the actor of it the extraordinary vengeance of God, and which is condemned not only by Scripture but even by the light of nature and the judgment of heathens who have expressly censured it as a great sin, and

as a kind of murder. Of which see my Latin Synopsis. Whereby we may sufficiently understand how wicked and abominable a practice this is amongst Christians, and in the light of the gospel which lays greater and stricter obligations upon us to purity and severely forbids all pollution both of flesh and spirit. 2. the cause of this wickedness, which seems to have been either hatred of his brother or envy at his brother's name and honour, springing from the pride of his own heart.

RAMSAY, FRANKLIN P. (1836- ?); Calvinist
Paraphrase of Gen. 38 --
9. But Onan knew that the offspring would not be his own; and so whenever he was with his brother's wife, he would pollute the ground rather than give offspring to his brother. What he did was bad in the eyes of Jehovah, and he took away his life also.

RICHTER, J. HEINRICH (1799-1847); Lutheran
In v. 9, shameful atrocities are designated that one does not want to mention! --Whoever practices this or something similar, things which from Onan have the name Onany [Onanism], cannot inherit the kingdom of God. 1 Cor. 6:9 and 10:8. Onan's behavior was punished by God with death because it happened contrary to the purpose of marriage and out of devilish jealousy and was also murder. Such silent sins always draw down the wrath of God. But even such atrocious sinners, of whom the world is now full, can still receive grace in the blood of Christ, if they come to Him in repentance; according to Tit. 3:3; Eph. 2:3.

RIVET, ANDRE (1573-1651); Calvinist
Commentary on Gen. 38:9 --
Now this is what Onan did and what happened to him in consequence. The cause which moved him to defraud his brother's wife and intentionally to deceive his parents was spite and envy. He could not openly reject his father's command, because he was even held to this by the common law. He considered the future offspring which Thamar would conceive not his own but his brother's, if he legitimately followed the custom with her. He abused the law of marriage in which he consented, and then exercised his lust, and under this pretext impurely contaminated himself, POURING THE SEED ON THE GROUND, neither did he provide posterity for his brother. We are limited from saying more about this by reason of modesty, but to pay it any attention at all: any abuse of the seed, especially voluntarily pouring it out outside of marriage, is a most serious sin: and it is necessary to guard against the suggestions of an impure spirit, with which Satan lies in ambush for many in the age

of adolescence and first puberty, whom he incites shamefully and effeminately to pollute and contaminate their own bodies..., corrupting themselves and inflicting a serious wound on their own consciences: which sin is most frequent among those to whom honorable marriage and the undefiled bed seem vile, among whom it is often found.

"He Who Himself Is Adulterer, Harlot, and Pimp"

Hence this is what the famous Jesuit, Scaliger, in his epistles often calls Onanism, from which he has frequently heard that this is what the apostle calls "malakian" [effeminacy; C.P.], 1 Cor. 6:9. Yet this was not properly the sin of Onan except in so far as he poured the seed on the ground. Therefore those who, by the same forbidden lust or violent abortions of offspring, destroy it before it is born, are like wicked Onan and involve themselves in the same type of crime and sin.

...For although every sin is evil and displeases God, they are still not all expressly said to be the same, so that some are more to be detested. That is even shown by the most immediate punishment, that God did not permit him to live any longer who deprived a generation of life and killed off the fetus in its own seed.

SCHMIDT, SEBASTIAN (1617-1696); Calvinist
Commentary on Gen. 38 --
Onan's act is most disgraceful and contrary to the order of nature. ...he seems to have done it not only out of jealousy toward his dead brother, but also and probably chiefly from greed, lest part of the inheritance be transferred.
Paul said earlier that to be evil in one's eyes is to displease mightily so that one just can't accept it. From this and from his speedy punishment (that is, death) the severity of the Onanitic sin is clear.

SCHRODER, FRIEDRICH W. J. (1817-1876); Reformed
Commentary on Gen. 38 --
-The seed has the promise of salvation - the promise on which the fathers grew. The levirate law was but a peculiar aspect, as it were, of that universal care for offspring which formed the Old Testament response to God's covenant faithfulness. Onan's sin a murder. It is as if the curse of Canaan descended upon these sons from a Canaanitish woman.

SCOTT, THOMAS (1747-1821); Anglican
Commentary on Gen. 38:9-10 --
V 9, 10. Onan's habitual conduct, (For this is meant,) was not only unnatural and detestable in itself, but full of envy and malice, and not without something of the nature of murder in it; for the same principle would have induced him to murder a child born to him but accounted his brother's, if he could have

done it with impunity. It implied also a contempt of the promise of a numerous posterity, made to Abraham, Isaac, and Jacob, and of that Seed especially in whom all nations "should be blessed".

The Scriptures sparingly hint at those vile practices, which, being done in secret, are a shame to be spoken of: this suffices to show, that the Lord notices and abhors them, and will bring to light all the lasciviousness, of which it is to be feared multitudes are guilty in heart and life, who stand fair in the world's esteem. Then the secret history of every individual, who hath not truly repented, and washed away his sins in the blood of Christ, will be written with an impartial pen, and published to the world of men and angels: every mouth will be stopped; and God's righteousness, in the condemnation of sinners, manifested to the whole universe.

SKINNER, JOHN (1851-1925)
Commentary on Gen. 38 --
Onan, on the other hand, is slain because of the revolting manner in which he persistently evaded the sacred duty of raising up seed to his brother. It is not correct to say (with Gu.) that his only offence was his selfish disregard of his deceased brother's interests.

STOCK, RICHARD (? -1626); Puritan
On Malachi 2:15 --
And so specially for the Church and increase of God's Kingdom: for though he can make children of stones, yet hath he ordained this means: therefore little reason and less religion hath the Church of Rome to prefer virginity before holy marriage; for besides that may be said to them, "It were better they would approve virginity by their deeds, than praise it by their words". And as Jerome [said]: "Why does the tongue sound out chastity, and the whole body show forth uncleanness?" Or, as Epiphanius [said] of the Origenists: "You refuse marriage, but not lust." It is not holiness but hypocrisy that is in honour amongst you. Besides this, virginity is never save only in some respect better than marriage, but marriage is oftentimes absolutely better than virginity, and by no reason more than this: because this may increase the Church, and bring forth sons and daughters to God, not that.

[The writing of Epiphanius (c. 315-402) on the Origenists, which Stock quotes, is about the deed of Onan, and is as follows: "There are some whom they call 'Origenians'. Which sect of humans is not spread everywhere, nevertheless this heresy comes in the next place after the above. But for what reason they are called 'Origenians' is not clear: Whether this was from Origen, as was said by Adamantius (who is known as Syntactes) or from some other? Because, as I said, I am completely ignorant, I have accepted nothing beyond the name itself. Their heresy truly conforms to the teaching of Epiphanes, about whom I have previously made sermons, against the sects of the Gnostics. They have cut out various books of the Old and New Testament. They repudiate marriage, but they do not refrain from obscene lusts, even to the point that they contaminate their bodies, minds and souls with every kind of filth. For certain of them profess the monastic life in appearance, and likewise their women prefer the same rule of life. All these have corrupted bodies, to the extent that when they satisfy their lust, they commit that crime, as I would more honorably call it, which Judah's son, Onan, is said to have committed. For when he used to have sex with Thamar, and satisfy his desire, he would do nothing for the propagation of children in the way it has been established for humans by God; instead he acted in such a way doing that shameful act that he brought injury on himself: So, the Origenians are wont to follow that old practice in regard to the things that are to be done for detestable lust. For they carry on not chastity, but the simulation of chastity to which they give the name falsely. Which action brings it about that, whatever woman is ravished, she does not get pregnant, or does not carry the foetus, so that nobody knows. Among them, by this their own rule of what they call chastity, they desire to maintain their prestige and reputation. And this worthless work of theirs is also a crime. But others carry on that wicked and shameful thing in other ways than with women: And they abuse themselves with their own hands for foul purposes. No less do they imitate the son of Judah, whom I mentioned; for by their nefarious sins and the distillation of their abominable fluid they pollute the earth. For they destroy their ejaculate on the ground lest it should be used for any procreation of a foetus."; C.P.]

TAYLOR, JEREMY (1613-1667); Anglican/Arminian
Rules for married persons, or matrimonial Chastity.
2. In their permissions and license, they must be sure to observe the order of nature, and the ends of God. "He is an ill husband, that uses his wife as a man treats a harlot," having nc other end but pleasure. Concerning which our best rule is, that although in this, as in eating and drinking, there is an appetite to be satisfied, which cannot be done without pleasing that desire; yet since that desire and satisfaction was intended by nature for other ends, they should never be separate from those ends, but always be joined with all or one of these ends, "with a desire of children, or to avoid fornication, or to lighten and ease the cares and sadnesses of household affairs, or to endear each other;" but never with a purpose, either in act or desire, to separate the sensuality from these ends which hallow it. Onan did separate his act from its proper end, and so ordered his embraces that his wife should not conceive, and God punished him.

THOMAS, W. H. GRIFFITH (1861-1924); Anglican Calvinist
Commentary on Gen. 38 --
We are not surprised that from this wicked association wicked sons should have sprung. The first born was so wicked that he came under the Divine displeasure, "and the Lord slew him". The second son was as bad if not worse, and was guilty of that sin to which his name has ever since been given, and of which it will suffice to say that it is perhaps the very deadliest of all sins as affecting definitely body, mind and soul, and as having slain its thousands in all ages of the world's history.

TRAPP, JOHN (1601-1669); Puritan
Commentary on Gen. 38:9 --
Ver. 9. WHEN HE WENT IN UNTO HIS BROTHER'S WIFE.]
God, for the respect he bears to his own institution of marriage, is pleased to bear with, cover, and not impute many frailties, follies, vanities, wickednesses that are found betwixt man and wife. Howbeit, there is required of such a holy care and conscience, to preserve between themselves, by a conjugal chastity, the marriage-bed undefiled; taking heed of an intemperate or intempestive use of it: which by divines, both ancient and modern, is deemed no better than plain adultery before God. He who lies with his wife, as if with a strange woman, is an adulterer, saith that heathen [Seneca; C.P.]. Onan's sin here was self-pollution, aggravated much by his envy that moved him to it, expressed in these words, "LEST HE SHOULD GIVE SEED TO HIS DECEASED BROTHER." And the more sinful was this sin of his in spilling his seed; because it should have served for the propagation of the Messiah; therefore the Lord slew him: as also, because he was not warned by his brother's punishment.

TUCH, JOHANN CHRISTIAN FRIEDRICH (1806-1867); Reformed
Commentary on Gen. 38 --
Out of misfavor against his brother, Onan knows how to keep the marriage unfruitful with the help of the vice named after him, and for that reason Jehova lets him die.

Onan indeed undertakes the levirate marriage, but the main purpose of it...(Ruth, op. cit.,) he knows how to evade through the acknowledged vice indicated in v. 9...and this sin brought God's punishment with it.

USHER, JAMES (1581-1656); Anglican/Calvinist Westminster Divine
On the Seventh Commandment --
How doth a man exercise uncleanness in act? Either by himself or with others. How by himself? By the horrible sin of Onan (Gen. 38:9), Lustful

dreams and Nocturnal pollutions (Deut. 23:10) arising from excessive eating and unclean cogitations or other sinful means (Jude 8, 2 Pe. 2:10, Gal. 5:19, Col. 3:5).

VENT, C. F. (1876)
The Crime of Onan --

But there is a practice so universal that it may well be termed a national vice, so common that it is unblushingly acknowledged by its perpetrators, for the commission of which the husband is even eulogized by his wife, and applauded by her friends, a vice which is the scourge and the desolation of marriage; it is the crime of Onan. "He spilled his seed upon the ground, lest children should be born. And therefore the Lord slew him, because he did a detestable thing"

Who can doubt that Almighty God, in this terrible punishment, wished to impart to man a positive moral instruction which should endure to the end of time, for the crime of Onan will have imitators while the world endures - as what crimes will not? But that these should be found among men of respectability would surpass belief, if the thing were not notoriously true. At any rate, the conjugal onanists in this age and country are more numerous than the exceptions. Ministers of the Gospel, prominent Church members, the very elite of society, well-nigh monopolize the art, for it is far less common to find repugnance to offspring in the lower classes than in "upper-tendom".

WESLEY, JOHN, (1703-1791); Methodist/Arminian
Commentary on Gen. 38:7 --

The next brother Onan was, according to the ancient usage, married to the widow, to preserve the name of his deceased brother Er that died childless. This custom of marrying the brother's widow was afterward made one of the laws of Moses, Deut. 25:5. Onan, though he consented to marry the widow, yet to the great abuse of his own body, of the wife he had married and the memory of his brother that was gone, he refused to raise up seed unto his brother. Those sins that dishonour the body are very displeasing to God, and the evidence of vile affections. Observe, the thing which he did displeased the Lord -- And it is to be feared, thousands, especially of single persons, by this very thing, still displease the Lord, and destroy their own souls.

WESTMINSTER ANNOTATIONS (1657); Calvinist
Commentary on Gen. 38:9 (by John Ley of the Westminster Assembly) --

The lewdness of this fact was composed of lust, of envy, and murder; the first appears, in that he went rashly upon it, it seems he stayed not till night, for the time of privacy for such a purpose, else the bed would have been named as well as the ground; the second is plain by the text, he envied at the honor of his dead brother, and therefore would not be father of any child, that should be reputed his, and not his own; the third, in that there is a seminal vital virtue, which perishes if the seed be spilled; and by doing this to hinder the begetting of a living child, is the first degree of murder that can be committed, and the next unto it is the marring of conception, when it is made, and causing of abortion: now such acts are noted in the scripture as horrible crimes, because, otherwise many might commit them, and not know the evil of them: it is conceived, that his brother Er before, was his brother in evil thus far, that both of them satisfied their sensualtiy against the order of nature, and therefore the Lord cut them off both alike with sudden vengeance; which may be for terror to those Popish Onanites who condemn marriage, and live in sodomitical impurity, and to those, who, in marriage, care not for the increase of children (which is the principle use of the conjugal estate) but for the satisfying of their concupiscence.

WORDSWORTH, CHRISTOPHER (1807-1887); Anglican
Commentary on Gen. 38:7 --
7. WICKED IN THE SIGHT OF THE LORD]. "The Hebrews and the Christians agree that Er committed the same kind of effeminate sin and retraction as Onan, which is contrary to the nature of procreation and marriage, for it destroys the fetus...and it is called destestable" (A. Lapide).

APPENDIX ONE

A LIST OF ADDITIONAL
PROTESTANT THEOLOGIANS
WHO OPPOSED BIRTH CONTROL

BAXTER, RICHARD (1615-1691); Nonconformist
BLOOMFIELD, SAMUEL THOMAS (1790-1869); Anglican
BRADFORD, WILLIAM (1590-1657); Pilgrim
BULLINGER, HEINRICH (1504-1575); Reformed
BUCER, MARTIN (1491-1551); Reformed
CARYL, JOSEPH (1602-1673); Westminster Divine
COMSTOCK, ANTHONY (1844-1915); Presbyterian
ENGELSMA, DAVID (Present day); Calvinist
EPISCOPIUS, SIMON (1583-1643); Arminian
FUERBRINGER, LUDWIG E. (1864-1947); Lutheran
GATAKER, THOMAS (1574-1654); Westminster Divine
GENEVA BIBLE (1608); Calvinist
GORE, CHARLES (early 1900's); Anglican
GOUGE, WILLIAM (1575-1653); Westminster Divine
GREENHILL, WILLIAM (1591-1671); Westminster Divine
HALL, ROBERT (1764-1831); Calvinist Baptist
LEIGH, EDWARD (1602-1671); Westminster Divine
MALTHUS, THOMAS ROBERT (1766-1834); Anglican
MANTON, THOMAS (1620-1677); Nonconformist
NAUMANN, MARTIN JUSTUS (1901-1972); Lutheran
OWEN, JOHN (1616-1683); Nonconformist
PINK, ARTHUR W. (1886-1952); Calvinist Baptist
POCOCK, EDWARD (1604-1691); Anglican
SPURGEON, CHARLES HADDON (1834-1892); Calvinist Baptist
ROBINS, JOHN B. (c.1896); Evangelical
ROGERS, RICHARD (1550-1618); Puritan
SAXONIAN CONFESSION
TAYLOR, FRANCIS (1590-1657); Westminster Divine
URSINUS, ZACHARIUS (1534-1583); Calvinist
WATSON, RICHARD (1781-1833); Methodist
WEEMES, JOHN (1579?-1636); Anglican
WUTTKE, ADOLPH (1819-1870); Protestant

Recently discovered:
DABNEY, ROBERT (1820-1898); Presbyterian
DODDRIDGE, PHILIP (1702-1751); Nonconformist
MACHEN, JOHN GRESHAM (1881-1937); Presbyterian

APPENDIX TWO
THE PILGRIMS AND A.W. PINK ON BIRTH CONTROL

THE PILGRIMS
(Recorded by Governor William Bradford, 1590-1657)
In the meantime, God in his providence had detected Lyford's evil carriage in Ireland to some friends amongst the company, who made it known to Mr. Winslow, and directed him to two godly and grave witnesses, who would testify the same (if called thereunto) upon their oath. The thing was this; he being got into Ireland, had wound himself into the esteem of sundry godly and zealous professors in those parts, who, having been burdened with the ceremonies in England, found there some more liberty to their consciences; amongst whom were these two men, which gave this evidence. Amongst the rest of his hearers, there was a godly young man that intended to marry, and cast his affection on a maiden which lived thereabout; but desiring to choose in the Lord, and preferred the fear of God before all other things, before he suffered his affection to run too far, he resolved to take Mr. Lyford's advice and judgment of this maiden, (being the minister of the place,) and so broke the matter unto him; and he promised faithfully to inform him, but would first take better knowledge of her, and have private conference with her; and so had sundry times; and in conclusion commended her highly to the young man as a very fit wife for him. So they were married together; but some time after marriage the woman was much troubled in mind, and afflicted in conscience, and did nothing but weep and mourn, and long it was before her husband could get of her what was the cause. But at length she discovered the thing, and prayed him to forgive her, for Lyford had overcome her, and defiled her body before marriage, after he had commended him unto her for a husband, and she resolved to have him, when he came to her in that private way. The circumstances I forbear, for they would offend chaste ears to hear them related, (for though he satisfied his lust on her, yet he endeavored to hinder conception.) These things being thus discovered, the woman's husband took some godly friends with him, to deal with Lyford for this evil. At length he confessed it, with a great deal of seeming sorrow and repentance, but was forced to leave Ireland upon it, partly for shame and partly for fear of further punishment, for the godly withdrew themselves from him upon it; and so coming into England unhappily he was lit upon and sent hither.

But in this great assembly, and before the moderators, in handling the former matters about the letters, upon provocation, in some heat of reply to some of Lyford's defenders, Mr. Winslow let fall these words, that he [Lyford; C.P.] had

95

dealt knavishly; upon which one of his friends took hold, and called for witnesses, that he called a minister of the gospel knave, and would prosecute law upon it, which made a great tumult, upon which (to be short) this matter broke out, and the witness were produced, whose persons were so grave, and evidence so plain, and the fact so foul, yet delivered in such modest and chaste terms, and with such circumstances, as struck all his friends mute, and made them all ashamed; insomuch as the moderators with great gravity declared that the former matters gave them cause enough to refuse him and to deal with him as they had done, but these made him unmeet for ever to bear ministry anymore, what repentance so ever he should pretend; with much more to like effect, and so wished his friends to rest quiet. Thus was this matter ended.

PINK, ARTHUR W. (1886-1952); Calvinist

Any teaching that leads men and women to think of the marriage bond as the sign of bondage, and the sacrifice of all independence, to construe wifehood and motherhood as drudgery and interference with woman's higher destiny, any public sentiment to cultivate celibacy as more desireable and honourable, or to substitute anything else for marriage and home, not only invades God's ordinance, but opens the door to nameless crimes and threatens the very foundations of society. Now it is clear that marriage must have particular reasons for the appointment of it. Three are given in Scripture. First, for the propagation of children. This is its obvious and normal purpose: "So God created man in His own image, in the image of God created He him: male and female created He them" (Gen. 1:27) - not both males or both females, but one male and one female; and to make the design of this unmistakably plain God said, "Be fruitful and multiply." For this reason marriage is called "matrimony," which signifies motherage, because it results in virgins becoming mothers. Therefore it is desirable that marriage be entered into at an early age, before the prime of life be passed: twice in Scripture we read of "the wife of thy youth" (Prov. 5:18; Mal. 2:15). We have pointed out that the propagation of children is the "normal" end of marriage; yet there are special seasons of acute "distress" when 1 Cor. 7:29 holds good. [1 Cor. 7:29 says: "What I mean, brothers, is that the time is short. From now on those who have wives should live as if they had none"; C.P.]

And now for a final word on our text. "Marriage is honourable in all" who are called thereunto, no class of persons being precluded. This clearly gives the lie to the pernicious teaching of Rome concerning the celibacy of the clergy, as does also 1 Tim. 3:2, etc. "And the bed undefiled" not only signifies fidelity to the marriage vow (1 Thess. 4:4), but that the conjugal act of intercourse is not polluting: in their unfallen state Adam and Eve were bidden to "multiply;"

yet moderation and sobriety is to obtain here, as in all things. We do not believe in what is termed "birth control," but we do earnestly urge self-control, especially by the husband, "But whoremongers and adulterers God will judge." This is a most solemn warning against unfaithfulness: those who live and die impenitently in these sins will eternally perish (Eph. 5:5).